A Collegiate Way of Living

A Collegiate Way of Living

RESIDENTIAL COLLEGES AND

A YALE EDUCATION

Mark B. Ryan

JONATHAN EDWARDS COLLEGE

YALE UNIVERSITY · 2001

This publication is made possible by the Jonathan Edwards Trust.

Designed and set in type at the direction of the Yale University Printer
Cover: The Great Hall, Jonathan Edwards College

© 2001 Yale University
ISBN 978-0-9723669-0-8

FOR GINGER
Who lived with me through it all
and who understood, celebrated, and shared in
my passion for it

Contents

Foreword by Richard H. Brodhead 9
Preface and Acknowledgments 11

Part One
THE EDUCATIONAL VALUE OF COMMUNITY LIFE
Introduction: Yale's Residential Colleges 17
Checking the Circles: Welcoming Remarks 25

Part Two
RESIDENTIAL COLLEGES IN HISTORICAL CONTEXT
The University: The Changing Shape of a Yale Education 35
The American Residential College: Genesis and Legacy 47
The Collegiate Way:
Historical Purposes of Residential Colleges 59

Part Three
ADVISING AND COUNSELING
Residential College Deanships:
An Anniversary Celebration 77
Self and Curriculum: Growing through a Yale Education 85
Inner Life/Yale Life 93

Part Four
ON COLLEGIATE VALUES: CRITIQUES AND COMMENTARY
The College in the University 99
Self-Knowledge and Liberal Education 113
Heart and Intellect: The Dalai Lama at Yale 129

Coda
Why J.E. Sux: The Spirit of a Residential College 143

Epilogue
Internationalizing Residential Colleges:
An Experience in Mexico 151

Foreword

A PERSON visiting Yale for the first time would be pardoned if he thought the residential colleges to be the school's oldest feature. Dignified with visible age—an admiring visitor once told me that he had not remembered that Yale had been built in the thirteenth century—the residential colleges dominate the central campus, giving Yale its distinctive look and spatial structure. In the undergraduate school, the colleges are at least as central to the spirit of the place as they are to its physical layout. Before they have been here one full day, arriving freshmen frequently identify themselves by saying "I'm in Pierson" or "I'm in Davenport" or "I'm in Morse." They identify with their residential college, this is to say. In the new identity they are forming as Yale students, their college affiliation holds pride of place.

The joke, of course, is that the colleges are not old at all. Seen within the whole sweep of Yale's history, they are in fact quite recent inventions. For fully three-quarters of its existence, from the founding in 1701 to Edward Harkness's proposal of the college system in the mid-1920s, Yale had no colleges, indeed had no idea of ever having them. (Harkness's offer to fund the building of the residential colleges, we can remember, was at first turned down.) In a world where the slightest innovation is talked out at endless length, it seems almost inconceivable that a school could ever have embraced the idea of consigning its whole future to this newfangled scheme, let alone cleared the ground on which to build it. But in the history of institutions, it would be hard to name a late interpolation that had made itself so central.

In the seventy years since their creation, Yale's residential colleges have continued to give undergraduates a pleasant, elegant place in which to live, eat, and associate. As their founders must have hoped but in ways they could scarcely have foreseen, they have also proved to be magnificently adaptable. Indeed the colleges have been crucial to this University's success at adjusting to new circumstances and embracing new functions. As Yale has grown in scale, they have taken on increasing value in giving students a small-college "feel" together with the resources of a great research university. When the colleges were created,

FOREWORD

Yale's concept of the services they should offer undergraduates was rudimentary in the extreme. But as Yale has come to embrace a fuller idea of service, the residential colleges have become the central site for individual student support, with the college deans—a position only half as old as the college system—giving aid and comfort on every front, academic, social, psychological, and even spiritual. Similarly, though they were built to house a relatively homogeneous student population, as the Yale undergraduate body has become radically more diverse, the colleges have become the chief site of education in the arts and values of community. The college suites and dining halls are the place where students learn to live together in the richest sense of the word, with comrades whose earlier lives may have nothing in common with their own.

No one, it may be, has a more intimate knowledge of the Yale residential college system than Mark Ryan. Having agreed to come in as acting dean of Calhoun College for one year in the mid-1970s, he served as dean of Jonathan Edwards from 1976 to 1996, a longevity unequalled in modern times. Long referred to as "the dean's dean," Ryan brought to this job virtues that this collection of writings brilliantly displays: unfailing grace of manner and expression, devotion to the college as both an ideal and a daily social reality, and an abiding concern for the whole human welfare of each student in his charge. Ryan brought a large measure of wisdom to this job, but he also learned by living and working so intimately with students, and this volume is the distillation of that knowledge.

One thing this volume teaches is that the residential college is a portable idea, something that has been carried from place to place since its inception in thirteenth-century Europe. In this light it is fitting that this great proponent of the college system should have left to give this idea new life in a new place. Ryan is now working to establish the first residential college system in Latin America, at the Universidad de las Américas in Puebla, Mexico. As he goes forward, he leaves us, together with the memory of his exemplary service, these reflections on what the residential college can mean. Seldom has anyone expressed so eloquently what this model of academic community can contribute to the development and education of the self. Along with our best wishes for his new collegiate ventures, he deserves our lasting thanks.

Richard H. Brodhead, *Dean of Yale College*

JANUARY 4, 2001

Preface and Acknowledgments

THE TEXTS in this volume emerged out of the life of Yale's residential colleges. Some were written as talks for the ceremonial occasions that are part of college life; others are broader reflections on the role that such residential communities play, or can play, in a university education. Together, they are an attempt to articulate the values and illustrate the functioning of a residential college system, and to portray its educational possibilities.

In classical political philosophy, there is a fundamental distinction between associations organized for "mere life," and those organized for the "good life." "Mere life" refers to the provision of basic physical necessities, whereas the "good life" implies the cultivation of virtue and human fulfillment—the full development of the talents and capacities of all individuals in the association. Essentially, that is the distinction between a dormitory and a residential college: a dormitory is organized to provide food and shelter; a college, to provide for the student's intellectual, social, and personal development. This book endeavors to show how residential colleges pursue those ends.

Yale's residential colleges and the similar house system at Harvard University were established simultaneously in the early 1930s with gifts from the same donor. They have since become models for residential systems or units established at universities across the United States and beyond. In recent years, as universities have grown in both size and a concomitant impersonality, more and more institutions, both public and private, have shown an interest in establishing or enhancing comparable, relatively intimate residential communities within their midst. It is my hope that the reflections gathered here might be of use in this growing educational trend.

Most of these essays and talks were written during my years as one of Yale's residential college deans, though many have been modified for inclusion in this volume. After a year as acting dean of Calhoun College, I accepted appointment as dean of Jonathan Edwards College, a post that I held from 1976 through 1996. By their influence on my own experience and perspective during my deanship and since, some colleagues have had an especially notable role in the genesis of this book. My wife Ginger Clarkson lived through most of those two decades with me, reflecting on its processes day by day, significantly affecting the college life with her own light and energy, and enriching my own perceptions with her insight into people and personal dynamics. She has also improved these pieces with her editorial suggestions. The late Horace Taft, then dean of Yale College, first appointed me to a deanship, and I remain grateful for his faith in me. Eustace Theodore, then dean of Calhoun College, and the late Martin Griffin, then dean of undergraduate studies, were especially instrumental in my training. I served under and learned from a succession of Yale College deans and masters of the college; all gave me, and my particular approach to the deanship, a support that enabled me to function happily throughout my tenure. The deans included Howard Lamar, Sidney Altman, Donald Kagan, and Richard Brodhead; and the masters, Charles Davis, Edgar J. Boell, Catherine Skinner, Frederic L. Holmes, and Bernard Lytton. I also had the benefit of shorter but valuable partnerships with three acting masters, Gary Haller, Martin Klein, and Murray Biggs. The master's spouse invariably plays a major role in college life (a role recently acknowledged by the title "co-master"), and my time in Jonathan Edwards was made all the richer by Millie Boell, Brian Skinner, Harriet Holmes, Norma Lytton, Sondra Haller, Linda Klein, and Lita Wright. My administrative assistant through most of those years, Heidi Kaminskas-Chagnon, kept our office humming with her receptivity toward and rapport with the students, just as she kept it sane with her unfailing sense of humor. To her and to Barbara Goddard, long-term senior administrative assistant to the master, I owe much. Joseph Gordon, successor to Martin Griffin as dean of undergraduate studies, was always a font of support and sage advice. My other colleagues in the Yale College Dean's Office, including many fellow residential college deans, are too numerous to mention here, but I have an abiding respect for and gratitude to them all. I also wish to thank my good friend Rabbi James Ponet, Jewish Chaplain at Yale, for all that I gained from our discussions of life at the University, and life in general. For the opportunity to apply my experience outside of Yale—and for the stimulation that they have provided in challenging me to rethink the essentials and the value of collegiate living—I am grateful to Enrique Cárdenas, Rector, and to Eduardo Lastra, Vice Rector for Student Affairs, at the University of the Americas in Puebla, Mexico. For their roles in ushering this book into publication, I am indebted to Penelope Laurans, Associate Dean of Yale College and Assistant to the President, whose encouragement was pivotal; to Lesley Baier, whose editorial talents significantly improved the manuscript; to John Gambell, University Printer, who generously gave of his time and talents in the book's design; and especially to Gary Haller, now Master of Jonathan Edwards College, and to the members of the Jonathan Edwards Trust, for their moral as well as material support.

Over the years, I served as residential college dean at Yale for some 2,500 students. In ways that they could never know, they were my teachers every bit as much as they were my students; and in the making of this book, I owe my greatest debt of gratitude to them.

Part One

THE EDUCATIONAL VALUE
OF COMMUNITY LIFE

The Great Hall, Jonathan Edwards College

Introduction

YALE'S RESIDENTIAL COLLEGES

When a multitude of young men, keen, open-hearted, sympathetic, and observant, as young men are, come together and freely mix with each other, they are sure to learn from one another, even if there be no one to teach them; the conversation of all is a series of lectures to each, and they gain for themselves new ideas and views, fresh matter of thought, and distinct principles for judging and acting, day by day.

JOHN HENRY NEWMAN, *The Idea of a University*, 1852[1]

IT WAS some seven years after their graduation when Melissa's closest friends from Yale gathered for her wedding, held in a Byzantine-style Catholic church in Manhattan, and then for the dinner and reception at the Boathouse in Central Park, decked in white and glowing with the light of tall, white candles. Since their Commencement ceremonies, the bride had gone on to a highly successful career as a Broadway actress, with the leads in two major musicals to her credit, as well as a role in a television series and exceptional critical acclaim for an actors' showcase. The groom was known in the sports world as a professional tennis player and television commentator, and notable and aspiring figures from both of those worlds—the stage and the courts—figured in the ceremony and feasted at the dinner. The warmth and exuberance that made Melissa such a compelling stage presence had attracted friendships throughout her twenty-nine years, but some of the closest ties in evidence among the revelers went back to her university days, and particularly to her life in one of Yale's residential colleges, the faculty-supervised undergraduate housing complexes that are designed to integrate living and learning. The matron of honor was her college roommate, and two of the bridesmaids were friends whom she came to know in the same college setting.

Seated at the dinner with still others of her Yale classmates, I saw ample evidence of the lasting impact that those residential college communities can have on students' lives. The colleges bring a grand diversity of bright and creative students into intimate contact, stirring their differing backgrounds, outlooks, academic interests, and individual enthusiasms into a piquant mix. The personal ties formed in those settings, accompanied by an often potent exchange of views, profoundly affect the students' education and can continue to educate them for years to come. When I first met Melissa, at a reception for newly arrived students in her freshman year, she recounted how her parents had first met at the piano in the college's common room, when her father was a student at Yale in the 1950s. Melissa's family background was Italian Catholic, steeped in the arts as well as medicine, and she had majored in art history. Her former roommate and current matron of honor was just as strongly Jewish, had studied economics, and was now involved in the world of development and finance. Undoubtedly their relationship had given each of them a window on the other's worlds, religious and professional, and on what in some respects were their very different ways of thinking.

At our table sat Peter, a composer, who recalled that his first musical play was produced in our college dining hall, under the sponsorship of a college drama group, with Melissa in a leading role. With Manoel and Abe, both of whom had been in the college, we reminisced about those days in New Haven and reflected in particular on the impact of college life. Abe was now an accomplished printer and graphic designer whose enthusiasm for that line of work had been spawned not so much by formal course work as by his tinkering with the letterpress in the college basement, creating signs and invitations for college-sponsored events. His closest friends in New York, he noted, continued to date from that college experience. Besides Melissa and Manoel, who himself now was a Broadway singer and actor, that group included Larry, who studied electrical engineering at Yale and now had his own Internet consulting company; Asa, a former English major who now worked in journalism as a writer and editor; Paul, who had studied astrophysics and now was in business; Matt, a photography editor for the Associated Press; and Tim, who managed computer databases for various corporations. Several of them were musicians on the side, and Tim, Matt, and Manoel continued to perform with a band that had formed back in the college. "I've been sitting around different tables with these people for ten years," Abe remarked, "sharing everything." As our conversation continued, Abe and Manoel recalled the abiding effect on them of one particular college-sponsored event, a visit to Yale by the Dalai Lama, where, seated on the floor in the close quarters of the master's living room, they found themselves mesmerized by the

INTRODUCTION

Tibetan leader's spirited and joyous presence. Manoel joked that he remembered my bright blue bow tie, the very one I was wearing that night, from formal proms in the college dining hall, when as their residential college dean, I with my wife used to surprise the students with our prowess on the dance floor.

College life encouraged a certain level of personal interaction between faculty and students as well as among students themselves; my own ties to the bride, for example, dated from counseling sessions on how she might juggle her pursuits in theater with the demands of her Yale education. Melissa and I had remained in sporadic contact since her graduation, but my invitation to her wedding, nearly a decade after those talks about reconciling a final exam schedule with rehearsals for "Les Miz," signaled something more than a certain level of generation-bridging friendship. To her, I suspect, and certainly to her friends gathered at that candlelit table, my presence was symbolic of, and testimony to, the lasting impact of that receding residential college experience on their lives.

* * *

As this book goes to press, Yale is celebrating its 300th anniversary. For most of the past century—almost seven decades of it—the residential colleges have been the defining organizational feature of student life there, imitated in varying degrees by other universities. At Yale and elsewhere, residential colleges are characterized by the presence of faculty, both as administrators and residents; by a sense of continuing tradition reinforced with ritual and symbol; and by organized student life in the form of student government, organizations, teams, educational endeavors, and social activities. In the complex environment of today's large universities, they draw together manageably sized groups of students, providing them a sense of home and a network of personal relations. Properly handled, they can immensely enrich the student's education: by reinforcing humane values, by providing ready access to consultation with faculty and other advisers, and especially by promoting a rich and relatively intimate contact among the students themselves, intensifying their ties to the university and enhancing what they learn from one another.

This volume draws on my twenty-year experience as dean of Jonathan Edwards College. Since it frequently refers to the life of that particular college in order to illustrate the broader principles and aspects of the residential college system, a brief description both of the system and of J.E., as the college is called at Yale, is in order.

Jonathan Edwards was among the first seven of Yale's colleges, which opened their doors in the fall of 1933. The original plan called for ten such colleges: the eighth opened the following year, the ninth a year after that, and the tenth in 1940. Two additional colleges were built in the early 1960s. Each of these units now counts around 400 to 450 undergraduate members, over eighty percent of whom are in residence. Students are assigned to the colleges shortly after their acceptance to the University, and before their arrival. All are made members of a college; no undergraduate students at Yale are unaffiliated with the system. Except in the case of "legacies"—the very limited number of students who might have a parent or sibling associated with a particular college—freshmen play no role in these assignments. So that the students might be exposed to the full range of the backgrounds and interests of their peers, the membership of each college is intended to be roughly a microcosm of the entire student body.

In only two colleges do freshmen live within the college quadrangle: most of Yale's first-year students live on the separate Old Campus. Nevertheless, their particular dormitories on the Old Campus are identified with a specific college and viewed as part of it. From the time of their arrival, they are fully members of their residential colleges: they take many of their meals in the college dining hall, participate fully in the college organizations and student life, and fall under the authority of the college administrators. Although policy allows students to transfer from one college to another, few do so: the vast majority maintain their original college affiliation throughout their four undergraduate years.

The chief officer of the college is the master, who at Yale is normally drawn from the ranks of senior, tenured faculty. He or she oversees the life of the college, the budget, and the fellowship of affiliated faculty, and—as the University would have it—attempts to set the college's "intellectual tone." The master is assisted in these matters by the dean, who also serves as chief academic adviser and personal counselor to the college's students, and who generally has a junior faculty appointment. Both the master and the dean live in the college, with their families: the master in a distinct master's house and the dean in a faculty apartment. Yale's colleges generally have two other faculty apartments, for resident fellows. Fellowships include senior and junior professors from across the spectrum of academic fields. They meet regularly, principally for social purposes, on a schedule that may vary from weekly to monthly, depending on the particular college. Many serve the college in other ways, particularly as advisers to freshmen; and some maintain their principal campus office within the college building. Additionally, a few graduate students—normally

INTRODUCTION

Jonathan Edwards College courtyard, September 1932

no more than two or three — receive housing and meals as remuneration for services provided to the college.

Jonathan Edwards College is named for the great Colonial-era philosopher and theologian, who graduated from Yale College in 1720 and subsequently served for two years as Tutor. It was designed in neo-Gothic style by the eminent architect James Gamble Rogers (Yale Class of 1889), who planned eight of the first ten colleges. Like its sister colleges, it is quadrangular in form, built around a landscaped courtyard; and it has as its focal interior space a large dining hall, which in this case is modeled after an Elizabethan banquet hall, with a soaring, beamed and gabled ceiling, dark paneled walls with intricate decorative carvings, a balcony, and two large stone fireplaces. Referred to in J.E. as the Great Hall, that space serves not only for dining, but for concerts, theater performances, dances, and other festivities. Also like the other colleges, J.E. is equipped with a sizable common room, for socializing and smaller assemblies, and with a senior common room for the fellows' meetings and dining. Both are lined with paneling and carving produced in the 1930s, largely by Italian craftsmen, and the fellowship takes no little pride in the eighteenth-century portraits by Joseph Badger of the Rev. Edwards and his wife Sarah that for decades have graced the senior common room, along with a desk and cabinets that purportedly belonged to Edwards himself. A junior common room serves as an additional, relatively intimate dining and gathering space. The college has two libraries, an original, smaller one that now holds periodicals, fellows' writings, and college memorabilia; and a larger one created in the 1960s out of an adjacent building previously occupied by the University's art department. Both serve as study and meeting spaces. The college houses three classrooms, about a dozen faculty offices, and five pianos (including one concert grand, for performances in the Great Hall). In its basement are numerous student facilities, including a computer room, a kitchen, a squash court, exercise rooms, a game room, a television room, a student-operated buttery, and such specialized facilities as music practice spaces, a darkroom, a woodshop, and even—as my friend Abe well knew—its own letterpress print shop. The spacious, three-story master's house is suitable for entertaining sizable groups of students and faculty; and the faculty apartments, with their large, paneled living rooms, are agreeable and roomy enough for both family life and entertainment of students.

With their grand neo-Gothic or Georgian-style spaces, these colleges certainly display the trappings of elite education. Yet the forging of collegiate learning communities is in no way dependent on such relatively lavish resources as are available at Yale. As I hope a subsequent chapter and the epilogue of this volume make clear, a collegiate way of living, while by no means cost-free, can be integrated into many different kinds of institutions.

Almost from the moment of their arrival, Yale students identify with their respective colleges. The vitality of their community life is expressed in numerous college organizations: student governments, intramural sports teams, music and drama groups, and committees dealing with social life and educational matters. A handful of residential college seminars—chosen by student committees, usually with the participation of some fellows—add a specifically academic component to college life. They are taught in the college's classrooms, and the college's students have priority in enrollment. The colleges, however, are social institutions. They are not identified with an academic field, and although the intellectual engagement that they promote is a vital part of Yale life, it is co- or extracurricular. The colleges are centers of academic counseling; they offer tutoring programs in writing and sciences and some noncredit, academically oriented programs such as senior essay workshops overseen by fellows. Prominent visitors occasionally deliver college-sponsored lectures or, more frequently, join in informal discussions at teas in the masters' living rooms. The dining halls and common rooms become the setting for plays, concerts, and other cultural events, often involving student performers.

INTRODUCTION

To the students, however, the most significant element of college life is less the "activities" than the strong bonds of friendship that naturally take hold in these close-knit communities. Such bonds are likely to form in any university setting, of course; but the residential college structure, keeping students in constant contact throughout their undergraduate years, is particularly effective in promoting them. "The really powerful friendships," observed Abe in our wedding-night conversation, "are formed within those walls." These personal ties, not only among close friends but also among ongoing acquaintances, undoubtedly contribute to the high level of student satisfaction at Yale, to the University's remarkable level of student retention (some ninety-five percent of entering freshmen earn a degree within five years), and eventually to the ongoing involvement of its alumni. "You feel like you're living in a small community," another of my students has explained, "even though you have all the resources of Yale. You don't feel lost. You're living with all sorts of different people, but you get to know them really well. You feel a shared spirit and energy, and that gives a sense of continuity."

The tradition of liberal learning has always viewed higher education as more than training for the marketplace, and the residential principle assumes that it is more than a training of intellect. A university exists to promote conversation — between generations, among teachers, and among students. Residential colleges form communities within the university, where the generations come together, where teachers of various disciplines converse with one another, and above all, where students freely mix with and learn from one another, over time — sharing their experiences, explaining their interests, inspiring one another with their enthusiasms. These social interactions, intensified by that "shared spirit and energy," help to stimulate the conversations that are the soul of a university. At the same time, the college's responsibility for student welfare, and the needs and arrangements of organized institutional life, assure that the university attends to the students' personal as well as intellectual development.

Surveying "living-learning communities" throughout the United States, Terry Smith has remarked that "Yale's is surely the archetypal residential college system in North America."[2] Melissa and her cohorts clearly benefited greatly by their presence in that system, by the conversation in which they engaged at Jonathan Edwards College. The setting in which that was so forcefully demonstrated to me — the Central Park Boathouse aglow with candlelight and reverberating with the revelries of people seen on stage and courts — surely had more than its share of glamour; but in vastly different kinds of settings, throughout the country and the world, alumni of the residential college system give testimony to the impact of that form of organizing a university society, and to the educational value of community life. This book is intended to portray why that is so. It attempts to depict the dynamics of the system, its historical roots, its underlying values, its potential, and, at least by implication, some of its possibilities beyond Yale.

If the pieces collected here are consonant in theme, they are admittedly heterogeneous in form. Some were written as formal articles about the college system, some as speeches and talks about its ideals and functions. Part One, besides presenting an introductory picture of the residential college system, is intended to highlight one of its most fundamental advantages: the way students in the colleges educate one another. Part Two explains the history and evolution of the college system—in the larger context of higher education in the West, in American universities, and at Yale in particular. It explains the theoretical purposes of college life, and the ways that Yale and other institutions have attempted, over the years, to enhance its advantages. A basic function of the college system is the advising and counseling of students; Part Three explores that enterprise and offers suggestions about how to conduct it. While my belief in the value of the college system, and of a Yale education, should be clear from the first pages of this book, I have certainly had my concerns about aspects of the education offered by modern elite research universities. In the spirit of a loyal critique, Part Four argues that the implicit educational ideals of the college system should be carried further than countervailing institutional patterns and practices currently allow; it calls for a greater emphasis on "collegiate" as opposed to "university" values. A Coda, in the form of a farewell talk, speaks of the communal spirit of college life. Finally, an Epilogue tells of the implantation of a college system, one modeled on Yale's, at a university in Mexico. It suggests the value of the collegiate ideal, not only beyond Yale, but beyond the Anglo-American systems of higher education. The enduring and transcendent value of that ideal is the central argument of these pages.

---

1 John Henry Newman, *The Idea of a University Defined and Illustrated* 1 (London: Basil Montgu Pickering, 1873), vi, 9. The lectures composing Part I of Newman's great work were originally delivered in 1852.

2 Terry B. Smith, "Integrating Living and Learning in Residential Colleges," in *Realizing the Educational Potential of Residence Halls*, ed. Charles C. Schroeder and Phyllis Mable (San Francisco: Jossey-Bass Publishers, 1994), 253.

Checking the Circles
WELCOMING REMARKS

Every year, over a hundred new freshmen arrive at each of Yale's residential colleges. The college administrator's challenge is to quickly make them feel at home there, to encourage them to be fully open to their fellow students, and thus to begin to mold this widely disparate collection of newcomers into a coherent community. What follows is the text of a welcoming speech, given as a post-dinner talk to a class of entering students in Jonathan Edwards College. It gives, I hope, a picture of the variety of students attracted to Yale and the range of their talents, provides a window into the life of the colleges, and indicates some of the fundamental values encouraged by the college system.

WE'VE GOT TO GIVE credit to Gregory Marsh, of this entering class in Jonathan Edwards College. Greg knows in his bones the limitations of the ways that we categorize people, the abstractions we create in our minds and on our bureaucratic forms to present ourselves to the world and explain others to ourselves. Specifically, I refer to your housing forms—those blue sheets you sent us last May, intended to indicate your preferences in a roommate. They have, you may recall, little circles that you were asked to check, telling us whether you go to bed early or late, whether you might be compulsively neat or irredeemably swinish, what kind of music batters your eardrums—and which of those habits you could tolerate in the room.

Staring at those empty circles and gothically imagining the possible consequences of checking one or the other can sometimes precipitate a crisis of identity or ethics. We might, for instance, question the mind-state of the person among you who told us that she goes to bed both early and late and would be upset with a roommate who does either; or the self-image of the person who said that she stays up late, is unusually neat, and plays both classical and rock in the room: she would be upset, she told us, if her roommate stays up late, is unusually neat, and plays both classical and rock in the room. Or consider the moral struggle of the person who first checked that she would be upset if her roommate were unusually neat, but then crossed that out with a note saying, "I am withdrawing my disapproval. Neat people are just fine."

Then there is Greg. The rest of you, for the most part, were content to do what we asked, and check the circle. Greg would do no such thing. He crammed reams of qualifications in the margins in four-point Garamond type. Does he go to bed before midnight? I quote his response:

> This is really hard to tell in advance. I usually go to bed from 11 to 1 at home, even on weekends, but that's because I live in a freakin' howling wilderness thirty miles from even the feeblest excuse for civilization. If I had serious work to accomplish the following day..., I'd probably be in bed by midnight, but I can guarantee nothing. Once I'm in skankin' New Haven, I may become some sort of nocturnal carpet-knight.

Is Greg unusually neat or sloppy?

> I'm neither neat nor sloppy to a degree I would define as "unusual." My clothes may or may not get folded, but they usually make it into a closet or drawer, and I do laundry at least once a week. I'm anally neat with regard to a few personal possessions, but cavalier about things like dusting.

And how does he feel about prospective roommates?

> "Unusually neat" is no problem, as long as the roommate hasn't got a muzzily Fascist mind-set that makes him yearn to spread his conception of purity beyond his own boundaries. "Unusually sloppy" is open to interpretation; I don't mind someone cultivating a sartorial sculpture-garden on his side of the room (that's his business), but unrestrained fungal growth in the bathroom disquiets me.

"I imagine," Greg adds, "that you're growing progressively more and more enthralled with my nebulous qualitative answers to this theoretically simplistic check-the-box section." Greg's point, of course, is that all of our ways of typing people have only a limited value, that we cannot assume too much from them, and that living in community requires that we look well beyond them, that we look far deeper into the souls and personalities of which they are only pale reflections. Or so, at least, I take as his point, since it is the point that I wish to address tonight.

That is not to say, mind you, that those categories are meaningless, be they about sleeping habits or about more profound and formative matters such as

place of origin or ethnicity. Far from it. They can point to real differences in our identity and loyalties and in our experience of the world. And they certainly tell us about the properly vaunted diversity that, over and over again, you have heard you will confront in Yale College and in our own particular college community. Let me, then, present you with some of them.

There are 110 members of this arriving Jonathan Edwards class; of those, fifty-four are women and fifty-six are not. You come to us from 105 cities, towns, and boroughs scattered over twenty-six states, the District of Columbia, the Commonwealth of Puerto Rico, and Canada, Ecuador, France, Germany, Denmark, Luxembourg, India, South Africa, and the People's Republic of China. You represent virtually all of this country's recognized categories of ethnic groups—embracing, for example, heritages of Cherokee, Creole, and Native Hawaiian. Some of you with American addresses now came originally from more far-flung territories and were born in Haiti, the United Kingdom, France, Israel, Russia, Slovakia, New Zealand, Indonesia, Hong Kong, Taiwan, Korea, China, and Vietnam. You are citizens of almost all of the places I have mentioned—thirteen countries besides the United States. In your homes is spoken, besides English, twenty-four languages and major dialects, including Spanish, Ladino, French, German, Danish, Polish, Russian, Slovak, Creole, Hawaiian, Hebrew, Turkish, Indonesian, Hindi, Urdu, Punjabi, Gujrati, Tamil, Korean, Vietnamese, Mandarin, Cantonese, Taiwanese, and Shanghainese.

Another aspect of your diversity is your range of academic interests. I might note that, of those of you willing to declare probable majors at this stage, twenty-nine opted for fields in the humanities, sixteen for the social sciences, and fifty-two—almost half—for natural sciences or mathematics.

It is, though, in speaking of your interests, your intellectual and other passions, that we most confront the truth of Greg's observation. It is there that your full individuality and personal diversity pour forth in ways that could never be predicted by any of those preconceived categories into which you might fall. Collectively, you speak of your love of creative writing, filmmaking, musical theater, and oil painting; of ballet, jazz dance, and flamenco; of singing and playing piano, cello, violin, guitar, flute, clarinet, tenor saxophone, and handbells. You speak rhapsodically about the elusive inner experience of writing poetry, of solving a mathematical problem, of making a computer program run faster and better.

You tell us of dancing the lead role of Titania in "A Midsummer Night's Dream," working to preserve the London home of the poet John Keats, of your intellectual struggles with the writings of Yale literary critic Harold Bloom, of sensing music as a religious experience with your a cappella group's performance of the medieval "Prayers of St. Francis" by Poulenc. Among you are people who have developed a system to analyze the stock market, who have applied the Laplacian method to calculate the orbit of an asteroid called "704 Interamnia," and who have taken a laboratory researcher's singular if not rather kinky joy in stimulating the sexual reproduction of sea urchins.

Athletes among you write ardently of the ways you have been shaped by the challenge and the competition, of the transporting feeling of that last surge of adrenalin in a ten-kilometer race. You are adepts not only in major team sports, but in such pursuits as karate, judo, figure skating, equestrian events, mountain biking, fly fishing, and rock climbing. Others hear the call of the earth: from exploring the ecosystem of the Florida Everglades, to trekking in the Sangre de Cristo Mountains of New Mexico or listening to the nighttime cries of loons and coyotes in a remote Maine wilderness. Community service looms large in your consciousness, through such works as peer counseling; emergency medical care; volunteering in a retirement home or an institute for the blind or a school for the retarded; experiencing a homeless shelter from the inside, overnight, as a client would; teaching for a year in South Boston; or founding an organization to fight bonded child labor on the Indian subcontinent.

Sometimes your individualistic pursuits struck me as hovering on the edge of the exotic: one of you confessed to having once watched fifteen movies in one week, another to collecting rare Barbie dolls. Still another says that he's into "Hitchcock [films], Leone westerns, teenage-hoodlum movies, punk rock and garage/surf/ska/lounge music (ancient and modern), plastic toys and their cartons from the '80s..., firearms, knife-throwing, and casual weight-lifting." You acknowledged compulsions for Mr. Bean, blueberry pancakes, *Mad Magazine*, and Tabasco sauce; for comic books, silk underwear, venomous snakes, and sharks.

What has brought such a collection of unique and spirited individuals to Yale from such a richly varied range of backgrounds? "Why, your stellar reputation, of course!" That's how one of you answered that question on our application form. But the reputation, it seems, means different things to different people. Some of you have a rather unique perception of it. "I first became interested in Yale at a rather young age," one wrote, "when I read that a disproportionately large number of employees of the CIA in its early days were culled from Yale. Nathan Hale was a Yale grad also... Not that I think Yale is a spy academy, exactly, but the abovementioned points lend it a certain unique cachet." Or here is a slant that not many of us could share: "Since childhood, my great-grandmother Susan Ann Morse Edwards has told the story of my family's verbal history in which I am presumed to be related to Samuel F. B. Morse and Jonathan Edwards. Learning that they had attended Yale University and that two of the residential colleges carried their names increased my interest in exploring Yale." I should say so.

More typically, you took note of Yale's attention to undergraduate education, its opportunities in the arts, theater, music, and community service, and its established excellence in particular fields ranging from English and history to molecular biophysics and biochemistry. Many were drawn by other Yale students, impressed by what one of you called the "intelligence, energy, and diversity" of students you met here, and by their enthusiasm and open love of the school. A number of you, I'm pleased to say, mentioned the residential college system and what one of you called the "heightened sense of community" that the colleges bring to student life.

Well, that brings me back to Greg's observation. Allow me now to take it one step further. In this residential college system, with its "heightened sense of community," all of that individual experience of your classmates that I've alluded to—that immensely rich range of heritage, interests, tastes, and skills—becomes available to each of you through the bonds that you will form in the college. Glance around this room and you may well see someone who in a short while you will think of as among the most important figures in your life. Your gaze surely will take in others who will introduce you to entirely new realms of experience, who might even reveal some new pathway in the landscape of your own destiny. For that to happen, of course, you must be open to it—and open, certainly, to them. As Greg reminds us, you will have to look beyond the category that you may first put them in; you will have to strive to understand their differences from you, to discover their mysterious complexities, to revel in their unique individuality—and at the same time to see reflected in them those basic qualities of humanity that unite us all.

That is a skill that I know you already possess. It is clear from your own writings, so let me merely reflect back to you some of your own wisdom. Your application essays tell us of your willingness to reach across wide gulfs of difference: they tell us of the revelations that have come to you when, for a clear and memorable moment, you became fully open to life as experienced by cultures or individuals that first seemed inaccessible. You tell us, for example, of the powerful experience of participating in a sweat lodge on a Northern Cheyenne reservation in Montana; of awkwardly entering a Shiite shrine in Syria; of communicating through chant with a group of Maori from New Zealand; or of spending your life on a bridge between American and Chinese worlds. You tell us of the profound lessons you absorbed from your friendship with an exchange student from Finland; from Jorge, a severely retarded but irrepressibly exuberant kid in a wheelchair; from a blind flutist's devotion to music; and from helping an eminent neighbor with Alzheimer's disease edit his memoirs in his last months of lucidity.

In those clear moments, of course, you find yourself plunging beyond assumption and difference to confront fundamentally human characteristics that all of us share. You find yourself plunging into a realm, if this does not sound too pompous, where we all seek happiness and endure suffering. To take Greg's lesson a step further is not only to recognize but to feel deeply that we all inhabit that realm — in ways that we might never predict from any boxes or circles that you have checked on a form.

At their most profound, your applications take us into that realm in your own lives, with an eloquence that would allow all of us to stand with you in joy or compassion, however extreme or unique your own particular experience may have been. You tell us why you felt supported and at home with your family, or why you did not; you speak of the rich bond among three sisters, of attending a birth, of taking in an adopted sister from Vietnam, of learning of your cultural past from a grandmother now in her nineties. You tell us, too, of more searing but indelibly formative experiences: living through a father's depression, your parents' bitter divorce, a mother's death from cancer, a brother's long and painful slide into schizophrenia, the final agonies of a beloved grandfather, even the murder of a best friend in his eighteenth year of life. You tell us how you were shaped by disappointing or sometimes frightening personal challenges: failing in a field at which a sibling excelled; being turned down for a seat in the city orchestra; having to support your own school expenses after a parent lost a job; moving to a new country at the age of eleven; finding yourself in a refugee camp in Thailand, or in the midst of the 1989 "Velvet Revolution" in Czechoslovakia, or trapped in the Crimea during the 1991 Russian military coup. You tell us of the long struggle to overcome a speech impediment, of the radical change in your life brought on by a rare blood disease. You speak of the depth and even the inspiration gained from coping with a congenital illness, or from that moment when in an automobile accident or in a coastal undertow you suddenly were brought face to face with the inescapable fragility of your own life. Sharing your own stories from your depths and with integrity, you tell us your sense of what it means to be human.

A former Yale president once wrote that the students educate each other fully as much as they are educated by the faculty, and that the residential college unit provides the most perfect setting for this process. If this is true—and I firmly believe that it is—it is because of the "heightened sense of community" that these colleges provide, and because you, the Yale students, rise to the challenge of living in them: by looking beyond those circles we check on our forms and in our minds; by being open to the wide range of experience represented by your diverse heritages; by cultivating, whatever your background, your unique individuality and supporting that of your classmates; and ultimately by experiencing your common humanity.

In that spirit, you find that by being true to yourself and your own experience, whatever it may be, each and every one of you has something vital to contribute to our common life. In that spirit, you create out of this neo-Gothic quadrangle the educational community of Jonathan Edwards College.

Thank you, Greg, and thank you all.

Part Two

RESIDENTIAL COLLEGES
IN HISTORICAL CONTEXT

1 A Front View of Yale-College and the College Chapel in New Haven, 1786

The University

THE CHANGING SHAPE OF A YALE EDUCATION

The residential colleges at Yale are shaped in part by the University's own institutional history. This is the text of a talk originally given to prospective students who had been admitted to the University "early action." It was intended to give them a sense of Yale by glancing at the changing form of education that the University has offered during its 300 years, and by relating that story to the architectural setting that many were exploring for the first time.

SHORTLY AFTER you graduate, Yale will celebrate its 300th anniversary. You are invited to join an unbroken train of young men and women who for nearly three centuries have been coming to this very plot of land, beginning with a couple of acres on the corner of College and Chapel streets. They have been coming, over the generations, seeking lots of things—youthful adventure, companionship, freedom from their parents—but seeking especially, we like to think, the best in liberal education. What I offer you today is an idiosyncratic tour of that three centuries of educational experience, glancing at who those young men and women were, how they lived, and especially what they learned.

From today's global and multicultural perspective, the two colonial colleges of New England were founded by a very specific and peculiar religious sect, British protestant Calvinists of the seventeenth and eighteenth centuries— Puritans, they were called. Whatever its virtues and failings, that tradition lent itself powerfully to promoting higher education. We begin this story with the unpleasantry of looking northward, to Massachusetts. Listen to one of the most extraordinary statements of the American colonial experience, written by Henry Dunster, the first president of Harvard, in 1643:

> After God had carried us safe to New England and wee had builded our houses, provided necessaries for our livelihood, rear'd convenient places for Gods worship, and settled the Civil Government: One of the next things we longed for, and

looked after was *to advance Learning and perpetuate it to Posterity;* dreading to leave an illiterate Ministry to the Churches, when our present Ministers shall lie in the dust.[1]

"To advance Learning and perpetuate it to Posterity." Imagine *that* as a priority, in those circumstances: a struggling colony in what seemed a wilderness, only ten years old, with a total population of only ten thousand, barely having built basic shelter, its very survival always under threat—and in an era when, even in Britain, only a scant few attended a university. The key reason they felt that need was that the Puritan religion, and its form of worship, were text-based. The main task of Puritan ministers—unlike priests and shamans in more ritualistic religions—was to expound on scripture, and they could do that well and correctly only with sophisticated learning and trained minds.

The founders of Harvard and Yale shared many assumptions about education beyond this sense of its necessity. Their ideals can be traced back through the medieval universities of Europe to the academies of Greece and Rome. The classical world had developed the notion of liberal education—an education for the *liber*, the free citizen—intended both to transmit a cultural heritage and to inculcate a general intellectual competence and personal virtue or character. By Roman times, the means of doing this was seen as training in the seven liberal arts: grammar, rhetoric, logic, arithmetic, astronomy, geometry, and music. Those arts, the Puritans still believed, were proper training not only for ministers, but for secular leaders as well. As Yale's founding charter put it, this was to be a place "wherein Youth may be instructed in the Arts and Sciences...[and] fitted for Public employment both in Church & Civil State."[2]

The Puritans had one other notion that turned out to be crucially important for the history of American higher education. "It is well known," stated Harvard's governing board in 1671, "what advantage to Learning accrues by the multitude of persons cohabiting for scholasticall communion, whereby to actuate the minds of one another, and other waies to promote the ends of a Colledge-Society."[3] The simplest way to "instruct youth" would have been to hire instructors, maybe rent or build some lecture rooms, but otherwise let the students make their own way in the town, living wherever they might. That was the way it was often done on the European mainland and in Scotland. But the Puritan magistrates wanted a *residential* college, where students learn together by living together. This was an especially English ideal, realized in the colleges that made up the universities at Oxford and Cambridge. There, students studied, lived, and worshiped in communities with their teachers—and they would do the same at Harvard and Yale. In that way, education became not merely a training of mind or a preparation for profession, but a comprehensive experience meant to develop character, to develop the whole human being in all its dimensions—intellectual, moral, personal.

With this place established up north, then, why was Yale necessary at all? People in Connecticut wanted their own college; but more than that, they grew convinced that up there in Cambridge the job had been botched. Listen to the Rev. Solomon Stoddard, preaching a sermon in 1703: Harvard, he said, was a place of "Riot and Pride... profuseness and prodigality... [It is] not worth the while for persons to be sent to the Colledge to learn to Complement men, and Court women."[4] In case you didn't get that seventeenth-century rhetoric, Harvard, he said, was out of control. Around the Yard they were listening to noxious characters like Episcopalians and showing far too much tolerance for non-Calvinist teachings. So in 1700, ten ministers gathered in Branford, Connecticut, to talk about founding a new college. Most of them were disgruntled Harvard alumni who, like alumni everywhere, thought their school had gone to the dogs since their own graduation. The Collegiate School, as it was called, was officially launched in 1701 with a charter granted by the colony's General Assembly, and with the intention to turn out "a succession of Learned and Orthodox men."[5]

In 1717, the school acquired this site by the green in New Haven, then a town of just some 1,000 souls. It gave the name Yale College to the first building it erected there, in gratitude to a benefactor with an exceedingly good sense of timing. Through mere usage, the name soon got transferred from the building to the school itself. In the middle of the eighteenth century the college added a more substantial brick structure, Connecticut Hall, which still stands as the oldest building on campus. Shortly thereafter a chapel went up beside it (fig. 1).

Now suppose you were coming to Yale not today, but two and a half centuries ago. What would the experience have been like? In the first place, there would be not 1,300 people in your class, but more like twenty-five or thirty, all of them, of course, men—or rather boys, as the entering age was typically about fifteen or sixteen. The entire student body would have numbered something over 100, and the faculty would have consisted of the president, one or two other professors, and three or four junior tutors. To be admitted, you would have had to pass an oral entrance exam, in front of the president, showing that you knew Latin and basic Greek, as well as rules of arithmetic. Not only were you to *know* Latin, mind you: it was the language of the College. You were expected not only to read your textbooks in it, but to speak it, both in and out of the classroom. Use of English was originally against College regulations, although we can't say how well that was observed. The requirement that students study Latin, by the way, lasted well into this century. In the 1920s, the Faculty almost abolished it; but the University's most eminent alumnus, former president William Howard Taft, who was on the Yale Corporation (the Board of Trustees), declared, "Over my dead body!" Taft had foresight. He died in 1930. The Latin requirement went with him in 1931.[6]

For all four years, at colonial Yale, each of you would have studied exactly the same things, together; and together you would have gone through the rituals of daily prayers and readings from scripture. The methods of learning were quite different from today. Like now, you would have heard lectures, but you also would have engaged in things called recitations, disputations, and declamations. A recitation was a parroting back of what you had memorized in a textbook; a disputation was a debate, in which you showed your command of the material by taking one side or another of a proposition, arguing for or against it according to the prescribed rules of logic; and a declamation was an oration, a lecture of your own that you embellished with the tropes of formal rhetoric. It was a far more oral form of learning than we have today, emphasizing memorization and eloquence.

The use of Latin shows another basic notion in the colonial New Englanders' concept of education. Their intention was not only to inculcate protestant orthodoxy, but to perpetuate the intellectual tradition of Europe, with its grounding in the classics. What you studied at Yale and Harvard was basically the same as what you would have studied all over Europe: the seven arts, some classical literature, plus what was known as the "three philosophies"—natural philosophy, ethics, and metaphysics. The Puritans saw no tension between promoting religious orthodoxy and perpetuating classical learning; in fact, they saw them as necessarily going together. In their view, classical learning prepared the way for Christian truth. To bring that truth to America, they had to bring the learning. It is all nicely symbolized in the two compatible buildings—college and church—in this print (fig. 1). But in fact, there was a tension there, because in the intellectual culture of Europe, those arts and philosophies were always growing and changing. Soon their growth began to threaten the orthodoxy; eventually, it threatened classical learning itself. There was a built-in tension between the Puritan goals of advancing learning, and perpetuating it to posterity.[7]

THE UNIVERSITY

2 Brick Row in the 1820s

Let's jump ahead now to the Yale of the early nineteenth century. Those two brick buildings had grown into what was called the Brick Row, with new buildings similar to the old, alternating the shape of a chapel with the shape of a secular hall (fig. 2). In this era, Yale was the largest college in the country, and the most national: by 1835 Yale College had some 400 students — about as many as one of today's residential colleges — and another 150 were enrolled in schools of medicine, law, and theology. The faculty had grown to include the president, five or six other professors, and ten tutors and instructors, a total of some sixteen. Yale had also become the mother of colleges: before the Civil War, Yale graduates had founded colleges across the midwest and south, and more than fifty had become college presidents. Parents might be interested to know that from 1815 to 1856, more than forty years, the cost of tuition held steady at $33 a year.[8]

As much as the College had grown in size and influence, the world of learning had grown still faster. Whole new fields had grown up, especially in the form of experimental science. In 1802, Yale appointed the brilliant Benjamin Silliman as its first professor of science — his title was Professor of Chemistry and Natural History. By the 1820s, the curriculum had expanded beyond the classics

39

to include chemistry and geology, more mathematics, English composition, optional courses in modern languages (including French, Spanish, and German), as well as "political economy," the beginning of social science. And English, you'll be glad to know, was the language of instruction.

All of this growth, however, precipitated something of a crisis, at Yale as elsewhere, because every student was expected to cover it all. There was still a single course of study that every member of an entering class was expected to follow for all four years: more subjects had simply been added to it. Moreover, pressure was growing from outside the schools to drop the classics altogether in favor of vocational training. Under President Jeremiah Day, Yale responded with one of the most important documents in the history of American higher education. It is known as the Yale Report of 1828—"the magna carta," as historian George Pierson called it, "for American liberal education."[9] The purpose of a college curriculum, it argued, was not to provide professional training, but rather to establish a firm basis for ongoing education. It was not to give specific, practical information, but to train the mind for a lifetime of learning, to impart habits of thought and judgment that subsequently could be applied in any field, and to give a broad purview of human thought and culture that could help make its students leaders in any profession. That has remained the sense of purpose at Yale ever since.

In another way, however, the report clung to ideals that could not last so long. It maintained that its goals were best fulfilled by a common, four-year course of study based on the classics, as well as by the old methods of instruction. Adding new fields to that common course had reached a saturation point: students could no longer absorb any more without sacrificing too much depth. Yet the study of science and other fields was growing even stronger, and their importance could not be denied. The temporary solution was to establish a separate program for students who wanted to pursue science. The School of Applied Chemistry, which later became the Sheffield Scientific School, opened in 1847. It was segregated from the rest of the College, two blocks away, on the corner of Prospect and Grove streets—the beginnings of the massive complex that we now call Science Hill.

Closer to Brick Row, to house its growing collection of books in many fields, Yale built a new library, its first stone building, in 1842 (fig. 3). It is still there, the University's second oldest standing building, known today as Dwight Hall. Take a close look at that building, because it embodies changing ideals and, I would say, the beginning of Yale's growth into an American university. It was modeled after King's College Chapel at Cambridge University. The pretensions of a university were coming to be symbolized by permanent, stone architecture in grand, Gothic styles, arranged in quadrangles like those at Oxford and Cambridge. Intellectually, those pretensions implied an expanded student body, more fields of study and facilities, and graduate programs and professional schools.

By the Civil War, both intellectually and architecturally, Yale was growing into just such a place. To the earlier schools of medicine, law, and divinity, it had added schools of science, engineering, and fine arts. The building we are now in, Street Hall, was originally the School of the Fine Arts, erected in 1866, the first such school in the country and the first school at Yale to admit women. These various schools included graduate programs, and in 1861 Yale granted three Ph.D. degrees, the first to be awarded in the country. In 1872, the Yale Corporation declared that Yale had "attained to the form of a University."[10] By then it had over 500 undergraduates, and some 400 more students in other schools,

3 Dwight Hall, today home to Yale's undergraduate Center for Public Service and Social Justice

taught by some twenty faculty. With a major building program, it had also begun to look like what people thought a university should, with Gothic buildings arranged in a quadrangle, stretching around the periphery of what we now call the Old Campus, and surrounding the more humble Brick Row, which except for Connecticut Hall was eventually torn down. By the turn of the century, the quadrangle was complete and appeared largely as it does today. Since the 1930s, it has been the domain of the freshman class.

With this growth into a university came changes in what students learned and how they learned it. Little by little, they gained more choice over what to study. The only way to accommodate additional fields of study was to let students choose from among them, with what were called electives. By 1900, about half of what a Yale student learned was prescribed, the other half elective. The educational philosophy that we stand with today had begun to take hold: the notion was that in the modern era, a proper liberal education consists of distribution and concentration. That is, it entails a broad experience of different forms of study, different ways of knowing, as well as the experience of depth, an advanced level of attainment in some particular field of knowledge. Shortly thereafter, concentration came to be defined as a major in one of the departments of study. In this era, too, the latter nineteenth century, old forms of learning like recitations and disputations were replaced by discussion seminars, written examinations, and research papers. Yale became a great center for scholarship in the humanities, and its lecture halls reverberated not just with the faculty's reading and commentary on textbooks, but with their original ideas and syntheses. Students flocked to hear spellbinding lecturers such as the legendary William Lyon Phelps, renowned professor of English, whose thoughts and voice may have filled this very room. From the time of Phelps's first lectures in the 1890s until today, Yale has had a magnificent tradition of magnetic lecturers, stretching to the likes of professors Cleanth Brooks in English, C. Vann Woodward and Jaroslav Pelikan in history, and Vincent Scully in the history of art—all of whom have been named Jefferson Lecturers by the National Endowment for the Humanities.

This was also the time when the extracurriculum in American colleges began to take the shape that we have known in the twentieth century. Colleges began to compete against each other in athletics, and from 1870 until 1910, Yale was (if you can believe it) the dominant national power in intercollegiate sports. With Harvard, Princeton, and Columbia, it formed the first Intercollegiate Football Association in 1876 and, through its great coach Walter Camp, formulated the rules of the game. That athletic legacy you will find not only in Yale's extensive sports programs, but in such facilities as the Yale Bowl, which opened in 1914, and the massive Payne Whitney Gymnasium.

This was the time, too, of the greatest prestige of a curious institution that had appeared before the Civil War, but that later grew significantly: the elite "class societies," Yale's early version of fraternities, such as the senior society Skull and Bones. Exclusive as some of those institutions were, the dominant tone of undergraduate life was what was then called "Yale democracy": the measure of a student was determined not by his social background, but rather by his character and by what he brought to College life. He could display his virtue in athletics and in activities such as writing for the *Yale Daily News*, the nation's oldest daily college newspaper, which began publishing in 1878; acting with the Yale Dramatic Association, which began in 1900; and singing with the Whiffenpoofs, the first of the a cappella singing groups, which was formed a few years later.

The recasting of Yale into a university was not met with universal enthusiasm. President Noah Porter, who held office when Yale declared itself a university, expressed grave reservations about what such a change had meant at other institutions. Above all, he wanted to preserve the focus at Yale on liberal rather than vocational education, and on the formation of good moral character. That commitment may be symbolized in the erection of the grand Battell Chapel on the Old Campus in the 1870s, during Porter's reign. Porter's ideal of education was to produce "Christian gentlemen," and he is often viewed as an irredeemable conservative. But the concern at Yale that he represented, the concern for the whole formation of the individual undergraduate, was an ancient Yale impulse, and a healthy one. In the early years of this century, America's new and mighty industrial wealth helped make this a world-class university—by international, not just American standards, a great center of research and of diverse graduate study. But concerns such as Porter's meant that the growing University never lost the sense that in Yale College, the liberal education of each undergraduate—his personal and ethical as well as intellectual welfare—remained at the heart of Yale's mission.

The specifically Christian element in that mission had steadily ebbed since the eighteenth century, as the University had become more and more secular. Porter's successor was the last Yale president to be a minister, and mandatory attendance at daily chapel services was abandoned in 1926, ending a tradition over two centuries old. Other elements of the ideal, however, survived in Yale's

4 Harkness Memorial Quadrangle

monumental effort, despite its growth, to remain a residential community where students learned not only in the classroom, but in close association with one another and the faculty. In 1917, across the street from the Old Campus, work began on Harkness Memorial Quadrangle (now Branford and Saybrook colleges), dormitories designed by the great builder of twentieth-century Yale, James Gamble Rogers (fig. 4). In the extraordinary years of the 1920s and '30s, under Rogers's architectural direction, Yale took the physical shape that it has today, constructing great emblems of its eminence as a university, such as the Sterling Memorial Library, the Sterling Law Buildings, and the Hall of Graduate Studies. But the Yale ideal was not to be just a university, but rather a "university college" that retained its focus on the undergraduate.

The benefactor Edward Harkness commissioned Rogers to create a whole system of intimate communities—residential colleges—inspired by those of Oxford and Cambridge. In these small communities, despite the growth of student numbers—which in 1930 stood at over 3,000 undergraduates and 2,000 in the graduate and professional schools—Yale would continue to cultivate those ancient ideals of collegiate living: ideals such as ethics, character, citizenship, friendship, and learning from one's peers. In 1933, the first seven of Yale's twelve

THE UNIVERSITY

5 South court of Berkeley College

residential colleges opened their doors: here is a preliminary drawing from Rogers's office of one of them, Berkeley College (fig. 5). The most recent colleges, Morse and Ezra Stiles, opened in 1960.

Since that time, the social background of the people who occupy these buildings has enormously diversified. In 1963 the University determined to meet the financial need of any student accepted in a need-blind admissions process, a measure that enlarged the pool of applicants and shifted the balance of students toward those who come from public rather than private schools. In 1969, after an abortive attempt to merge with Vassar, Yale College admitted women for the first time. About the same time, an effort was funded to recruit students from underrepresented ethnic groups—motivated by a principled belief in equal opportunity and a drive to tap academic talent that otherwise might not have come. Today, Yale's 11,000 students come from all over the nation and the world to study in a dozen different schools of the University. The 5,000 undergraduates of Yale College study under some 800 faculty, recognized for their advanced level of research in more than forty fields of study.

We warmly invite you to join them. We invite you to join that long, unbroken train of young men and women who for three centuries have been coming to this ever-changing and expanding plot of land, seeking the best in liberal education. If you come, I hope that you can do so with some awareness of the generations that have preceded you, and that have contributed to making this institution a place that can immeasurably enrich your life. As you walk around the campus, I hope that you'll think, from time to time, of the Puritans who believed so fully in the importance of higher education; the generation of Jeremiah Day, who defined the enduring values of liberal education; the active visionaries who helped make of this old college a great American university; the restless undergraduates who created the energetic extracurricular traditions of Yale life; the nostalgic alumni who perpetuated some virtues of the old Yale in a unique system of residential colleges; and the recent alumni who have given the Yale of today such a lively, multicultural face. All of those generations are joined in the enduring effort, first articulated on American shores so long ago and interpreted, even on this one plot of land, in so many ways, but still standing as our principal purpose: "to advance Learning and perpetuate it to Posterity."

1 Henry Dunster, "New England's First Fruits" (1643), reprinted in Samuel Eliot Morison, *The Founding of Harvard College* (Cambridge: Harvard University Press, 1935), 432–44 (italics mine).

2 Cited in Richard Warch, *School of the Prophets: Yale College, 1701–1740* (New Haven: Yale University Press, 1973), 31.

3 Cited in Samuel Eliot Morison, *Harvard College in the Seventeenth Century* 1 (Cambridge: Harvard University Press, 1936), 49.

4 Cited in Warch, 18.

5 Cited in ibid., 31.

6 Frederick Rudolph, *Curriculum: A History of the American Undergraduate Course of Study since 1636* (San Francisco: Jossey-Bass Publishers, 1977), 214.

7 This interpretation is pursued by Warch.

8 George Wilson Pierson, *A Yale Book of Numbers: Historical Statistics of the College and University, 1701–1976* (New Haven: Yale University, 1983).

9 George Wilson Pierson, *Yale: A Short History* (New Haven: Yale University, 1976), 35.

10 Cited in Brooks Mather Kelley, *Yale: A History* (New Haven: Yale University Press, 1974), 242.

The American Residential College
GENESIS AND LEGACY

PERMIT ME to begin, for the sport of it, with one Harvard man bashing another. Here is Charles Francis Adams, writing in 1909 to Woodrow Wilson, then president of Princeton, looking back on the forty-year reign in Cambridge of Charles William Eliot, the president who not only remade Adams's alma mater but launched American higher education into a new era: "I consider that Eliot has, by his course and influence, done as much harm to the American college as he has done good to the American university."[1]

Adams's brotherly barb came at a crucial historical moment, when the values of the old American residential college were being revived in the prestigious institutions of the East after forty years of erosion during the movement, epitomized by Eliot, to build the great American university. Soon would begin the effort to reestablish the residential college, with its educational purposes and values, within the context of the newly built and more broadly defined university. That polarity in Adams's statement, between "college" and "university," would likely confuse most of the American public, which tends to use both terms, often interchangeably, to refer to institutions of higher education. But my purpose is to reflect on the historical roots and educational meaning of that polarity, and to advance a few thoughts about what it might mean to universities today.

* * *

In their origins, both terms referred not so much to place and institution as to societies or communities—specifically, to the medieval guilds of masters and students that carried on the function of teaching and learning, and whose organization, regulations, and acts of incorporation are the roots of the modern university. Both terms, then, implied a recognition that teaching and learning are social endeavors, naturally pursued in a community of teachers and students. By the fifteenth century, however, *universitas* had come to signify a place of higher learning, an institution, more than the people who carried on its functions.[2] The term college, stemming from the Latin *collegium*, indicating a partnership or organized social group, retained a more social connotation. Although it too became associated with institution and place, it continued to denote a society of scholars.

"College" had multiple uses, but it was eventually applied to some of the residential groupings, usually organized as charitable trusts, that had begun to appear in medieval university towns, often for the purpose of housing impecunious scholars. The early universities of Europe provided no lodging; but students clearly required it, and benefactors saw a need for structured social institutions to provide for young scholars in body and soul. What later became known as the *Collège de Dix-huits* was founded in Paris as early as 1180. By the end of the fifteenth century, Paris was host to some seventy such institutions, and they had appeared in other university towns across Europe.[3] The most lasting and substantial, however, were in Britain, beginning with Oxford's Merton, University, and Balliol colleges, all established in the thirteenth century.

Adams's forebears, the Puritan magistrates who founded his alma mater, may have rather grandiosely named that miserable little burg where they put their school after the great English university that several of them had attended. But the model for the school that they had in mind was not the multifarious collection of institutions by the River Cam, but rather the collegiate units within it. The colleges they had known at Cambridge—Emmanuel, Trinity, Christ's—had grown up first as mere boarding houses, but had then gradually gained ascendancy as centers of teaching and learning.

Perhaps the earliest permanent residential college, still extant, was Merton of Oxford, founded in 1264 by the Bishop of Rochester to take care of the "temporalities," as he said, of students—and perhaps not incidentally, to assure the good behavior and proper development of his nephews. The buildings of Merton were grouped around a chapel, where students worshiped daily; its statutes, establishing the seminal "Rule of Merton," prescribed diligence, sobriety, chastity, and other personal virtues. Merton and its early imitators were not teaching institutions, but with the founding of New College, Oxford in 1379, older fellows of the college began instructing younger ones. By the middle of the next century, the teaching functions at Oxford and Cambridge lay almost entirely in the hands of college lecturers.[4] Unlike the university, the colleges governed student life beyond instruction: they attempted, we might say, to manage a student's full development.

That was the model that the magistrates of Massachusetts Bay had in mind when they set out to build an institution "to advance Learning and perpetuate it to Posterity." Some of the more practically minded observers suggested that the school simply hire ministers to read lectures, leaving the students to fend otherwise for themselves. But as Cotton Mather later retorted, "the Government of New England was for having their Students brought up in a more Collegiate Way of Living."[5] From that beginning in Massachusetts Bay, American higher education was concerned not only with the training of minds but also with the molding of character, and the "Collegiate Way of Living," with its common residence, structured community life, intellectual exchange, and spiritual purpose and practices, was the path to those complementary goals.

To support the Collegiate Way, the early colonial institutions—reflecting their passion for this ideal—erected the largest buildings in the English colonies: Old and New colleges at Harvard, the Wren Building at William and Mary, Nassau Hall at Princeton.[6] In those ambitious structures were a hall for lectures and dining, a kitchen, a buttery, a library, and chambers for students and tutors. There students heard lectures together; demonstrated their mastery of ideas through recitations and disputations; followed a rigorous daily discipline of prayers and study, meals and recreation; and in their intellectual and personal development, pursued for four years in close community, formed lifetime bonds with one another.

Mind you, not everyone in the colonies was pleased with the results. Conservative ministers such as Solomon Stoddard attacked Harvard for its licentiousness, and the London agent for Massachusetts and Connecticut complained that the College was "bringing up a strange generation there."[7] He threw his support to the new, rival school in Connecticut. But there, as in succeeding institutions founded in colonial times, and in the rash of college-building in the early nineteenth century, founders still chose to bring up new generations in the Collegiate Way.

* * *

Perhaps the most notable formal defense of this collegiate ideal, at least prior to the Civil War, emanated from that place in Connecticut, which originally had been called the Collegiate School. The focus of the seminal Yale Report of 1828 was curricular: it defended the classical curriculum—the study of what was called "the dead languages" and mathematics—as well as a prescribed, common study of other subjects chosen by the faculty. But it also defended the close community and residential arrangements of the traditional American college. The young students of that era needed, in the words of the report, "a substitute...for parental superintendence...founded on mutual affection and confidence" between students and their teachers. "The parental character of college government," the report stated, "requires that students should be so collected together, as to constitute one family; that the intercourse between them and their instructors may be frequent and familiar."

That goal, the report noted, required suitable residential structures and resident faculty who knew the students individually and well. These arrangements allowed not only for providing information to students through lectures—what the report called the "furniture" of the mind—but also for the "daily and vigorous exercise" of what it called the "mental faculties," on which it based its educational psychology. The intellectual exchange in the community, then made formal with daily recitations and disputations, was a crucial pedagogical tool. The aim of all this—both curriculum and college life—was "to lay the foundation of a superior education" and, as the report stated it, to "produce a proper symmetry and balance of character."[8]

Take note here that the rationale for the residential college had moved, over two centuries, from one that was primarily spiritual—protecting the moral welfare of the students—to one that was more psychological: encouraging students' full human development, both intellectual and personal. The rationale remained, as before, focused on the student, but it was grounded now less in a theological understanding of human nature than in human psychology as it was then understood. Educators of that era found this rationale convincing: graduates of these institutions in the East set out to found colleges across America, until by the eve of the Civil War there were some 250 of them, many aspiring to the educational ideals of the Yale Report. The residential ideal was reinforced by an American habit of placing these schools in rural settings—often in towns with names such as Athens and Oxford—away from the temptations of the cities, where other living arrangements would have been available.

* * *

Nevertheless, this collegiate ideal had a fundamental weakness. From the beginning, it had been associated with a common curriculum, and even a unitary view of knowledge. That curriculum was derived from the early Renaissance reconciliation of classical learning with medieval Christian theology, in which every intellectual endeavor had its place in a larger framework. The intellectual history of American higher education can be viewed as a progressive breakdown of that unitary view of knowledge, under the pressure of secularization, new perspectives, and new fields of inquiry.

By the time of the Yale Report, that process had begun to tear at the very structure of the American college. The explosion of new knowledge from Europe, especially in the sciences, had begun to crowd the curriculum, making it seem cursory, or to antiquate it, making it seem irrelevant. Democratic, newly industrializing America wanted more practical, vocational subjects; and an educational elite, looking at the intellectual advances of Europe, called for the study of modern languages, political economy, and the blossoming diversity of natural sciences. Such subjects could be incorporated only if students could *choose* from among various course offerings.

With the attack on a common curriculum often came an attack on the close-knit community life associated with it. Reformers such as Francis Wayland, president of Brown, took as their model not the old English colleges but the very different nonresidential universities of Germany, with their emphasis on independent and graduate study and on faculty research. Wayland called for the study of new subjects, an elective system, professional and vocational study, and — striking at the heart of the old college — for the abolition of residences and of the college's role in "parental superintendence." Without the burden of residences, he argued, the school could devote its resources to academic purposes, to professorships and libraries — with the added benefit that students might not so readily lead each other to moral perdition (a point that some of us who live among them must, I'm sure, from time to time entertain).[9]

These thoughts did not bear fruit until the flowering of the university movement after the Civil War, funded by the new wealth of American industrialism. By the 1870s, great public universities and land-grant colleges had begun to rise in the Midwest, built to accommodate a much-expanded university population and a more service-oriented, utilitarian curriculum. Johns Hopkins was founded as a graduate research institution on the nonresidential German model; and, fortified by an elective curricular system, greatly expanded universities began to emerge out of some of the old colleges. Frequently, these creations and expansions entailed the abandonment not only of a prescribed curriculum, but of chapel, community rules, and dormitories.

The great spokesman for the expansion of the old American college into the new American university was Eliot of Harvard, who assumed his post as president in 1869 and kept it through the first decade of this century. At the heart of Eliot's reform was the elective system—free choice from a wide range of course offerings. He built his case on a radical individualism: because students were not uniform, he argued, neither should be the curriculum. It must not only change with new knowledge and social conditions, but it must allow for wide variation in tastes and talents—for, as he put it, vast "diversities of...minds and characters." Eliot was a pluralist: he wanted a large student body, studying widely varied fields and drawn from "different nations, states, schools, families, sects, parties, and conditions of life." In part, this was so that students could educate each other about their various backgrounds. But his more compelling reasons were institutional: they concerned the faculty he wanted to cultivate. Without a great many students, "numerous courses of highly specialized instruction will find no hearers." Electives and a large student body freed the faculty to concentrate on areas of specialization. They were the necessary conditions of what Charles Eliot defined as a university.[10]

For Eliot, building the university implied deemphasizing the residential nature of the American college and its supervision of student life. A large university could not, as he phrased it, seclude students "behind walls and bars." He favored urban campuses, with many students living in the city. If the sense of the college as a close community suffered in the process, so be it; community was not his goal.[11]

In terms of the future definition of American higher education, Eliot prevailed. The university ideal triumphed—and of course not only at Harvard. New fields of inquiry and legions of new students were accommodated in expanding institutions all over the country—including even more traditional places such as Princeton and Yale, where Eliot's ideas had initially been viewed with horror. As Eliot noted, "The manners and customs of the Yale faculty are those of a porcupine on the defensive."[12] In one of the more vitriolic debates among American college presidents, Noah Porter of Yale and James McCosh of Princeton attacked Eliot's university pretensions, defending prescribed study and the supervision and moral guidance of students in residential halls. Referring to the relinquishing of institutional control over students' behavior and course of study, McCosh fumed, "if we cannot avert the evil at Harvard, we may arrest it in the other colleges of the country."[13] But even at his and Porter's own institutions, electives increasingly took over the curriculum, and a smaller proportion of resources went into the building of dormitories. The residential, collegiate ideal was clearly in retreat.

THE AMERICAN RESIDENTIAL COLLEGE

* * *

By sometime during the first decade of the twentieth century, however, a backlash took hold. Many—the likes of Charles Francis Adams—were not enamored of increased specialization, with its focus on research rather than teaching and on graduate and professional schools instead of undergraduate education. They had profound reservations about an unstructured undergraduate curriculum, about the laissez-faire attitude toward student morals and character, and about the separation of intellect from other aspects of development. The collegiate ideal began to revive within the new university.

A leading figure in that revival was Woodrow Wilson of Princeton. As university president, he spoke of the need to join "intellectual and spiritual life" and to "awaken the whole man." Princeton, he said, was "not a place where a lad finds a profession, but a place where he finds himself." Wilson moved Princeton away from the free elective system back toward a more structured curriculum; and with the construction of residences, he attempted to rebuild the sense of community that he thought the university had lost. "The ideal college...," he said, "should be a community, a place of close, natural intimate association, not only of the young men...but also of young men with older men...of teachers with pupils, outside of the classroom as well as inside of it."[14] For architectural inspiration, Wilson looked back once again to the English residential colleges with their closed quadrangles. Hiring Ralph Adams Cram, preeminent spokesman for the revival of the English Gothic style, as Princeton's supervising architect, Wilson hoped to create an entire system of residential quadrangles, each with a dining hall, common rooms, and a resident master. His notions culminated in the design and construction of the Graduate College, but he failed to win support for his larger vision.[15]

In the later 1920s, Alexander Meiklejohn created a short-lived undergraduate residential college at the University of Wisconsin. Designed as a two-year program of general education, his Experimental College housed faculty offices with student bedrooms in an attempt to create "a community of liberal learning."[16] But the fulfillment of Wilson's vision for a lasting and comprehensive system of residential quadrangles took place neither at Princeton nor Wisconsin: it awaited the philanthropy of Edward S. Harkness, Yale Class of 1897, who in 1926 proposed to fund such a system at his alma mater. Yale was slow to respond with a plan, and the delay tried the patience of the donor, who began to feel that Harvard might prove more fertile ground for his generosity. By that time, Eliot's notions were in retreat in Cambridge. His successor,

A. Lawrence Lowell, ally of Charles Francis Adams and admirer of Wilson, steered Harvard back to collegiate ideals with fewer electives, an emphasis on undergraduate teaching and what he called "cultural and spiritual values," and efforts to create a more close-knit community life. Harkness made the same proposal to Lowell, who snapped it up, calling it "a bolt from the Blue." After the announcement, a Yale undergraduate magazine referred to the scheme as "a Princeton plan being tried out at Harvard with Yale money." Harkness then reconciled with his alma mater and agreed to fund what was called the "Quadrangle Plan" at both schools.[17]

Harvard and Yale thus simultaneously mustered their considerable talents toward what must be viewed as one of the great enterprises in the history of American higher education: the creation of collegiate units *within* the modern university and, through that, the joining of collegiate and university ideals. Officials from both institutions went scurrying across the Atlantic to examine the Oxbridge colleges on which their new units were supposedly to be modeled. But what they needed to build, of course, was something quite different. The British colleges were autonomous sovereignties, self-governing and independently financed agents of instruction with their own faculties. The American units, grafted onto an existing, centralized university, would be something new, something between a British college and an American dormitory.

Thus began the enterprise to which today's residential colleges are the heirs. The initial phase was, I believe, a moment of inspired creativity. In fashioning these units, the planners at Harvard and Yale faced the fundamental issues shaping discussions today: issues such as the optimal size and architectural configuration of the units; their staffing; the functions of their officers; forms of faculty involvement; their educational as well as social functions; their relation to existing units of authority, especially departments of study; their relation to the extracurriculum; the forms of their student governance; and even such symbolic concerns as names, titles, and heraldry.[18] Since that time, Rice and the University of California at Santa Cruz have constructed comprehensive systems of four-year colleges, patterned largely after those at Harvard and Yale, in which all students are enrolled. Princeton has created a system of two-year colleges that may yet expand to four. In the economically flush years of the 1960s, universities such as Michigan State introduced residential colleges, often with an academic focus, as one among various available housing options. More recently, an array of universities including Pennsylvania, Virginia, St. Lawrence, Northwestern, Wisconsin, Southern California, North Carolina at Greensboro, and Northeast Missouri State have created some type of "living-learning" units.

* * *

Looking over this broad history of the collegiate tradition, we see two basic characteristics: that tradition accepts the educational value of community life, and it strives to develop the whole student psyche. In interpreting that legacy for our purposes, of course, we accept the enduring elements of the university ideal. From Eliot's day onward, the American university would be devoted to the advancement as well as the perpetuation of learning. It would have a faculty focused on areas of specialization. It would accept the reality that students come with vast diversities of minds and characters, requiring wide range in choice of study. It would draw its students from ever more pluralistic backgrounds—from, in Eliot's terms, "different nations..., families, sects..., and conditions of life."

But within that context, the residential college aims to promote the enduring elements of what Cotton Mather called "the Collegiate Way of Living." In promoting cohesive communities within the university, the collegiate ideal embraces the principle that informal contact in structured community life is a significant element in the learning process. We attempt to give meaning to the old ideal of mentorship, recognizing the value of what the Yale Report called "mutual affection and confidence" or "frequent and familiar intercourse" between students and faculty. Some modern commentators point with passion to that need. As Page Smith puts it, "there is no decent, adequate, respectable education, in the proper sense of that much-abused word, without personal involvement by a teacher with the needs and concerns, academic and personal, of his/her students."[19] This implies that a residential college should provide for a strong faculty presence—for formal and informal avenues of advising and counseling, of listening and affirmation.

The collegiate ideal also accepts the principle that students educate each other fully as much as they are educated by the faculty. They may absorb information in the classroom, but it is in exchanges with one another that students internalize that information, take the measure of what rings true, relate it to their experience and intuitions, and assess how it has meaning in their lives. Further, in their diverse backgrounds, tastes, experiences, and perspectives, they expose one another to sometimes infectious insights and interests, to rich if sometimes painful personal histories and experiences. The educational value of that exposure argues for college communities that reflect the full social diversity of the university population.

The second enduring element in the collegiate ideal is that it attempts to look after the whole student psyche, to promote the development of character as well as intellect. That is a persistent theme, from the Yale Report's psychological portrait of the student to Woodrow Wilson's concern that a Princeton student find not a profession but himself. The college must seek to create an atmosphere in which students are supported in their full personal growth. The college community supports that growth by serving as witness to it, by appreciating it, by providing a forum in which all student concerns—especially personal and developmental ones—can be given a full hearing. For college officers, this implies that what we might call human sensitivity is every bit as important a credential as scholarly achievement. College officers should be skilled as personal counselors, and they have an obligation to familiarize themselves with the major issues of personal development in the college years.

A traditional element in this focus on character in the collegiate ideal is an emphasis on values we call moral and spiritual. Obviously, that does not mean for us what it meant for Cotton Mather, but the terms crop up in the whole history of the Collegiate Way, through the rhetoric of Woodrow Wilson and Lawrence Lowell. Their meaning for us, I would say, is twofold: it lies in community ethics and in personal awareness. Ethical concern should be at the heart of the college's community life. In their interactions with each other, in the creation and enforcement of college regulations, students must constantly be encouraged to look to the community's harmony and welfare and to consider how the virtues and values that thus come to play are expressed—or not expressed—in the larger society.

As for the spiritual element, perhaps colleges in the modern secular university must be content to let it emerge from the bonds of affection formed in the group—and to encourage a place for inner, personal exploration. If the concerns that we call spiritual are rooted, as I believe they are, in compassion—in the cultivation of sincerity, mutual acceptance, even love—then they can be nourished in the ties and mutual understanding formed in college life. To make the most of that opportunity for spiritual growth, colleges must find ways to encourage in students a deepening awareness of personal experience, of what Vaclav Havel has called "trust in [one's] own subjectivity as a principal link with the subjectivity of the world."[20] Through that, they can encourage some attention to the life cycle, some concern for the largest context of human life.

In carrying forward these enduring ideals, we as heirs to the collegiate tradition can promote, in the fragmented university of today, a student-focused vision of education that, in a way appropriate to our times, both builds characters and sharpens minds. In so doing, we can help to make the modern university a place that answers the concerns of both Charles Francis Adams and Charles William Eliot—a place that reconciles the contrasting but compelling views of two Harvard men bashing one another.

This chapter is based on a keynote address given at the First Annual International Conference on Residential Colleges and Living-Learning Centers, held at Northeast Missouri State University in 1992. It was published as "Residential Colleges: A Legacy of Living and Learning Together," in *Change: The Magazine of Higher Learning* 24, no. 5 (September/October 1992), adapted for inclusion in *Gateways: Residential Colleges and the Freshman Year Experience*, ed. Terry B. Smith (Columbia: University of South Carolina Press, 1993), and reprinted in *Learning from Change: Landmarks in Teaching and Learning in Higher Education from "Change Magazine," 1969-1999*, ed. Deborah DeZure (Sterling, Va.: Stylus Publishing, LLC, 2000).

1 Cited in Laurence R. Veysey, *The Emergence of the American University* (Chicago: University of Chicago Press, 1970), 250.

2 See Francis Oakley, *Community of Learning: The American College and the Liberal Arts Tradition* (New York: Oxford University Press, 1992), 17.

3 Ibid., 20.

4 This account of the rise of the English colleges is drawn from Samuel Eliot Morison, *The Founding of Harvard College* (Cambridge: Harvard University Press, 1935), 35–39.

5 Ibid., 251–52.

6 Paul Venable Turner, *Campus: An American Planning Tradition* (Cambridge: The MIT Press, 1984), 17.

7 Richard Warch, *School of the Prophets: Yale College, 1701-1740* (New Haven: Yale University Press, 1973), 18, 59.

8 A Committee of the Corporation and the Academical Faculty, *Reports on the Course of Instruction in Yale College* (New Haven: Hezekiah Howe, 1830).

9 Francis Wayland, *Thoughts on the Present Collegiate System in the United States* (Boston: Gould, Kendall & Lincoln, 1842), 112–31.

10 Charles William Eliot, *Educational Reform: Essays and Addresses* (New York: The Century Co., 1898), 125-48.

11 Ibid., 147; see also Veysey, 93.

12 Cited in Veysey, 50.

13 James McCosh, *The New Departure in College Education* (New York: Charles Scribner's Sons, 1885), 23; see also Noah Porter, *The American Colleges and the American Public* (New York: Charles Scribner's Sons, 1890).

14 Veysey, 212, 242, 243.

15 See George Wilson Pierson, *Yale: the University College, 1921-1937* (New Haven: Yale University Press, 1955), 224; see also Turner, 227-34.

16 See Frederick Rudolph, *The American College and University: A History* (New York: Alfred A. Knopf, 1962), 477-78. Meiklejohn provided his own account of the college's purposes in *The Experimental College* (Madison: University of Wisconsin Press, 1928).

17 Pierson, 208. Pierson provides a superb and detailed account of the Harkness gift: see 207-52.

18 See especially ibid., 400-74.

19 Page Smith, *Killing the Spirit: Higher Education in America* (New York: Viking, 1990), 7.

20 Vaclav Havel, "The End of the Modern Era" (address at the World Economic Forum, Davos, Switzerland, 4 February 1992); excerpted in *The New York Times*, 1 March 1992.

The Collegiate Way
HISTORICAL PURPOSES OF RESIDENTIAL COLLEGES

THE COLLEGIATE WAY, it seems, is beckoning again. In an effort to enhance community life and improve student services, Columbia University has initiated a "house system," providing residential units with a resident dean and counselors, academic advising services, a library, computer facilities, some classrooms, and programs of dinners and discussions led by faculty and prominent visitors. With its new system of residential colleges, the University of Pennsylvania has taken a similar step; and well away from the Ivy League, Murray State University in Kentucky has also created an ambitious college system with similar structure and services. Northwestern, the University of Southern California, and the University of Virginia, to cite three salient examples, lately have expanded their residential college programs; Winona State and Northeast Missouri State, among others, have established new ones. Within the limits of their facilities and resources, such programs are modeled on the now venerable "house" and "college" systems of Harvard and Yale, created in the early 1930s and inspired, in turn, by the ancient collegiate structure of Oxford and Cambridge.

The newer programs join well-established systems or institutions not only at Harvard and Yale, but others created in the 1950s and 1960s, notably at Rice, Michigan, Michigan State, and the University of California at Santa Cruz. Most of these universities label their creations "residential colleges"; if other residential arrangements with an academic purpose—generally styled "living/learning centers," "theme houses," or "interest units"—are added to the picture, the sense of a revival becomes all the stronger. *The North American Directory of Residential Colleges and Living Learning Centers*, compiled in 1993 by Terry B. Smith and Elizabeth Raney, lists sixty-four schools that have such institutions.[1] About half of them, report Smith and Raney, began their programs since 1982. And that compilation, depending as it did on responses to questionnaires, makes no claims to be complete; already it is outdated.

Parallel movements have taken place in other countries influenced by British educational tradition: in Canada, Australia, and in Britain itself, from the University of Manitoba to the University of Wollongong to the University of Kent at Canterbury. A series of international conferences on residential colleges and living/learning centers was initiated in 1992. Literature on the subject, too, is growing: in addition to compiling the *Directory,* Terry Smith, who as dean of the colleges at Northeast Missouri convened the first conference, has edited a monograph entitled *Gateways: Residential Colleges and the Freshman Year Experience,* in which representatives of a number of institutions describe their particular programs. A recent volume edited by Charles Schroeder and Phyllis Mable entitled *Realizing the Educational Potential of Residence Halls* takes up the subject as well, notably in a piece by Smith. Internet sites now provide links to Web pages of residential colleges throughout the world.[2]

All of this activity, of course, raises questions of purpose and definition. The various colleges, centers, and houses noted in the *Directory* cover a broad spectrum: from James Madison College at Michigan State, which enrolls 1,000 students, houses 500, and grants degrees, to special-interest modules at, say, SUNY Binghamton, which might house as few as ten. While all are intended to enhance learning, some have a sharply defined academic focus; others do not. Some, as at St. Lawrence, are only for freshmen; others, as at Virginia, are primarily for upperclassmen. In his article in the Schroeder and Mable volume, Smith ventures a definition of the "classic" residential college: it is specifically intended to "supplement and enrich students' academic experiences," and it involves "faculty and students sharing living and working space." By those criteria, he counts approximately thirty schools with such institutions.[3]

Excluded from that count, of course, are the myriad private, degree-granting and largely residential small liberal arts colleges across the country. Smith is concerned with residential units in larger institutions. Both the liberal arts colleges and these residential units, however, stem from a common source. When, as president of Princeton, Woodrow Wilson first proposed a college system in 1906, and when the benefactor Edward Harkness volunteered in the 1920s to make such systems possible at Harvard and Yale, their stated hope was to revive virtues of the old colleges in the new and expanding universities that these schools had become. Even then, however, they had varying notions of what, exactly, those virtues might have been.

Goals of the current expansion of residential college systems may be even more varied. Often they are expressed in terms of the needs of a particular institution. When articulated more broadly, they may be expressed, rightfully, in terms of modern understanding of student development. This burgeoning of activity, however, also invites a sweeping look backward at the historical purposes of residential colleges. For such institutions, including independent liberal arts colleges, are at the heart of the peculiarly American contribution to higher education, traceable even to the founding of Harvard in 1636. And they afford a rich history, inadequately mined, that expresses enduring goals of residential life in higher education, and that can help us conceptualize the purposes of our own endeavors. My own survey points to six such goals: ethics, citizenship, community, instruction, cocurricular programming, and peer learning. In one form or another, each of these goals survives in our own measures of student need, and in our efforts to build residential college communities in the modern university.

Ethics · Initially, colleges arose as charitable trusts within the medieval universities of Europe, to provide small groups of scholars with basic needs of board and lodging.[4] They were most elaborately developed in England, where the founding of Merton College, Oxford in 1264 established a model for succeeding institutions. It was the colleges of Oxford and Cambridge, successors to Merton, that informed the early American notions of collegiate life.[5] The purpose of what Cotton Mather called a "Collegiate Way of Living" was, above all, moral. It was intended to promote a student's spiritual welfare and to guide his ethical development. Merton and its successor colleges—such as Emmanuel of Cambridge, the college of many of Harvard's founders—were built around a chapel, the center of daily worship. Elaborate rules—following the "Rule of Merton"—strictly structured a student's day, governed his behavior, and presumably disciplined his character. Formation of character even more than of intellect remained the purpose of most independent American colleges through much of the nineteenth century. The character thus formed was to be imbued with "Christian virtues." When, early in this century, Woodrow Wilson, then president of Princeton, and Charles Francis Adams, overseer of Harvard, proposed "quadrangle" or "college" systems within their respective universities, it was in part to counter what they saw as a growing neglect of this central collegiate function.

The rules of Emmanuel and early Harvard, of course, now strike us as puritanical in every sense of the term, and Wilson's and Adams's notion of a "gentlemanly ideal" rings anachronistic and perhaps elitist. It is this moral purpose of the historical residential college that, to us, can seem most alien. But the students' need for ethical formation persists, even at the modern secular university; and residential colleges continue, perforce, to address it. They do so for the very reason that in them students live together, in community. For their survival and their harmony, colleges require that students develop a respectful regard for one another, and for the community as a whole. They are therefore in a position to assume some responsibility for ethical development, even when that responsibility, as many see it, has been abrogated in the curriculum.

Faculty leaders of these communities are in a position to promote, explicitly, the virtues of a successful community life: mutual respect, tolerance, civility, compassion, responsibility, a sense of justice and of the common good. In the interactions of everyday life, those virtues are constantly put to the test; because the communities are small, their effects, and the effects of violating them, are constantly in evidence. The Rule of Merton may be long gone, but rules of some kind these communities must have, and their enforcement necessitates an appeal to—and thought about—basic human values. When rules are violated, faculty leaders are in a position to teach students about the principles that stand behind them. In a well-run residential college, the interactions, even the abrasions, of student life are not left alone: they provide opportunities for empathy, and for discussions and learning about value, purpose, and meaning. Students learn from one another's joys, pains, and traumas. If the small community can model ideals, and the adults associated with it model virtues, and if reflection on both is encouraged, then values are clarified and nourished.

The last few years have seen a growing awareness of students' need for ethical formation in the college years, and no shortage of laments that, in this respect, universities are neglecting a fundamental charge. James Laney, Parker Palmer, Page Smith, and Bruce Wilshire, among others, have called for a renewed attention to the university's role in helping students form a deeper sense of meaning, a personal set of values. It is certainly no accident that Professor Wilshire, one of the most sophisticated of these critics, calls as well for the creation of residential colleges, where "meaningful human lives" are modeled by resident faculty, where virtues are taught by the presence of people who embody them.[6]

Citizenship · Historically, the focus on ethics in residential life has been paternalistic, emphasizing the inculcation of virtues by an older and wiser authority. The Yale Report of 1828 spoke of a need for the college to provide "a substitute for... parental superintendence."[7] Such paternalism may have been fitting for a time in which the entering age of students was approximately fifteen. Later in the century, however, the strict structure of rules, and the enforced piety that went along with it, began to break down. In a movement led by independent colleges such as Amherst, the goal of "parental superintendence" gave way to an ideal of student self-governance. By early in the twentieth century, many colleges had surrendered some measure of authority and oversight to student governments. The rising notion was that students best learn to govern themselves, both individually and in community, by doing just that. Through exercising leadership and self-governance, students learn "citizenship" — participation in, and leadership of, organized community life.

As they arose near the turn of the century, official student governments were a compromise measure, a way of bringing hedonistic and sometimes violent elements of student life back under some measure of administrative supervision. Nevertheless, the ideal of cultivating "citizenship" in this way was genuine, and it persists today as a major goal of residential college life. Rice University, which in the late 1950s established one of the premiere systems in the country, states in its *General Announcements* that each of its eight undergraduate colleges "is a self-governing group of students" responsible for directing activities, appropriating funds, and "maintaining good order"; the goal is to foster among its members "a mature sense of honor, responsibility, and sound judgment."[8] Programs at several universities attempt to turn the sense of responsibility thus cultivated outward, as well, to the larger society. Describing the residential college at the University of North Carolina-Greensboro, an institution for freshmen and sophomores founded in 1970, Frances Arndt observes the evolution of "a complex system of student committees" overseeing all major aspects of student life. All residents are expected to serve in college governance in some way, and many participate in internships and volunteer programs off-campus, reporting on their experiences back in the college.[9]

Such student organizations, of course, are common at universities across the land. But by dividing large undergraduate populations into small, highly articulated communities, residential colleges provide many more students with the opportunity to participate in them in a meaningful way. With a student membership of barely over 400 students, Jonathan Edwards College at Yale, for example, boasts not only a student government, but a drama group, a literary magazine, twenty-seven intramural sports teams, and committees overseeing curricular programs, housing allocation, and social life. Each of them provides opportunities to assess needs, adjudicate differing opinions, mobilize participation, implement programs, and consider goals. A reassessment of Yale's college system, undertaken in association with its fiftieth anniversary in 1983, cited "taking part in activities for the common good, the ability to govern and be governed in turn," as fostering a "civic education." Such an education, it contended, was at the heart of what residential colleges have to offer.[10]

Community • By definition, of course, a college is a community, and the collegiate ideal has always emphasized the value of the social bonds that a college fosters among its members. The intimacy of ties among students, and between students and faculty, intensified by residence, has long been seen as promoting the students' personal as well as intellectual development. From colonial times (and long before) the intimacy of collegiate life has been the source of lifelong friendships. As Samuel Eliot Morison tells us, class bonds in particular "became one of the distinctive features of American college life."[11] Emphasizing ties between students and instructors, the Yale Report of 1828 employed the metaphor of a collegiate "family."[12] In the early twentieth century, after venerable American colleges had expanded into larger universities, it was the loss of that sense of community, as much as any factor, that gave rise to the drive to build residential college units within them. In promoting the notion at Princeton, Woodrow Wilson articulated his social goal of creating communities that would foster "close, natural, intimate association" among students and between students and faculty.[13] Though he was unable to realize his dreams for Princeton, the ground proved more fertile at Yale and at Harvard, where President A. Lawrence Lowell, friend and ally of Wilson, had suggested a residential college system even before taking office.[14] Like Wilson, Lowell spoke frequently of the value of community life. When the benefactor Edward Harkness, Yale Class of 1897, made the "Quadrangle Plan" possible at Harvard and his own alma mater, his purpose, according to Yale's official announcement, was "to revive amid the intellectual advantages of the great modern university the social advantages of the small Yale College of earlier generations."[15]

If there was need to revive a sense of community in the universities of the 1920s, there is an even greater need to do so in the much larger, more disparate, and certainly more impersonal institutions of higher education today. For good reason, the rhetoric of community, calling for smaller, more intimate associations of students, is prominent in more recent efforts to create residential colleges. The State University of New York introduced its residential college structure in 1968 to "reduce students' feeling of anonymity as the University began to grow into a major research institution."[16] The University of Southern California subsequently founded Dean's Hall "to create an increased sense of community at the university."[17] Officials in charge of Columbia's recently established experimental program describe it as an attempt to make the University "feel... small" and "to create a community."[18]

What such communities provide is a network of social connections that are centrally important to a student's experience of the institution. Through that network, the potentially jolting transition to university life can be eased, and a sense of a new home, with a ready-made circle of friends, quickly established. College-organized peer counseling programs for freshmen can be highly effective in that process, providing an immediate sense of institutional support and connection to the entire residential college community. The visible presence of college officials and affiliated faculty certainly works toward the same end. At Yale, the effects of this process are shown in students' immediate identification with their colleges: from the first days on campus, residential college affiliation is central to a student's sense of identity. Residential college officials and associated faculty then become a link to the entire university and its abundant but potentially confusing array of resources. Their adult presence is a constant symbol of institutional concern, even when students do not draw on it directly. More significantly, they are able to play a major role when students show signs of difficulty. The close-knit nature of these residential communities makes it unlikely that a student in personal turmoil will long be isolated. It enables early interventions that sometimes can be of surpassing importance in students' lives. In less dire circumstances, the ever more familiar adult presences in a college often aid students in working through personal questions and stresses. College officials have no more important role, I believe, than in their counseling.

Residential colleges can enhance the community life not only of students but also of faculty. The most established programs, following the British model, involve faculty fellowships that cross departmental lines, creating opportunities for dialogue and collegiality that circumvent an often rigidly departmentalized university organization. Kristine Dillon has found that in USC's program, "faculty have not only enriched the students' experience but have deepened their own connections by establishing collegial relationships with involved faculty from other disciplines."[19] For students and faculty, separately and together, residential colleges can answer to that "ringing call for the renewal of community" that Ernest Boyer and others have addressed to the academy.[20]

Instruction · In founding New College, Oxford, near the end of the fourteenth century, William of Wyckeham required older fellows to teach younger ones. In the middle of the following century, Magdalen College invited undergraduates to take both board and instruction in the college walls. Eventually, the colleges of Oxford and Cambridge, which initially had been units of living and worship more than formal instruction, assumed nearly all responsibility for teaching their boarders.[21] Elsewhere in Europe, such as at Sigüenza and Alcalá in Spain and at Trinity College, Dublin, some residential colleges assumed not only the responsibility to teach but the authority to grant degrees, becoming independent institutions of higher education.[22] The founders of Harvard, too, conceived of their college as a place of both residence and instruction; and that was the model for independent, degree-granting colleges subsequently founded throughout the colonies and the young American nation. By the late nineteenth century, many of those independent colleges had grown into multifaceted universities. Their student bodies had grown too large, and their instruction too varied, to fit the old model of living and learning in close-knit communities. Authority over instruction passed to the academic departments.

When Edward Harkness's generosity made possible the re-creation of collegiate units at Harvard and Yale, he and the officials of those universities looked again to the British model. It soon became clear, however, that they could not recreate the British system, in which colleges were autonomous units of instruction. Rather, they were grafting a collegiate structure onto existing, centralized universities, where authority over instruction already was clearly defined. The new houses and colleges were to be primarily social and residential units; instruction would remain the responsibility of academic departments.

From the start, however, those responsible for these colleges—recalling especially the British tutorial system—saw in them the potential for uniquely valuable modes of teaching. Residential colleges held the promise of creating true intellectual communities, where common exposure to ideas enlivened daily life, where thoughts originating in the classroom were developed in impromptu conversation, where teachers and students formed personal and intellectual bonds. Wilson envisioned the quadrangles that he hoped to create at Princeton as settings for "preceptorial," or small group, instruction.[23] In 1927, building on Wilson's ideas, Alexander Meiklejohn established the short-lived but widely touted "Experimental College" at the University of Wisconsin, the first undergraduate residential college to be reintroduced into a major university. Intended for freshmen and sophomores, it was an enterprise in general education, with a two-part curriculum focused on classical Athenian and modern American civilizations. The teaching faculty held offices interspersed among student rooms; all classes took the form of intimate group or individual discussion. Instruction was the heart of the enterprise: Meiklejohn even defined a college as "a group of people, all of whom are reading the same books."[24]

Though judged a success at Wisconsin, Meiklejohn's college lasted only five years. The more enduring creations at Harvard and Yale also found the collegiate structure to be at odds with preexisting departmental lines of authority, with pressures on faculty to answer first to their departments. That tension has limited the instructional function of these units, although they have continued with some teaching on a small scale. Over the years, their endeavors have included "early concentration" seminars for freshmen, sophomore-level general education seminars, section meetings of large introductory courses, and house or college seminars (sometimes taught by faculty emeriti, graduate students, or visiting professionals) on subjects not included in the regular curriculum.

Despite the limitations on it in these "model" systems, curricular instruction remains central to the rationale of many residential colleges. Sixty-four percent of programs included in Smith and Raney's *Directory* offer credit-bearing courses.[25] Some founded in the late 1960s and early 1970s—notably James Madison at Michigan State, the Residential College of the University of Michigan, and Unit One at the University of Illinois—are firmly curriculum-based.[26] Five actually grant degrees.[27]

The same independence of departmental authority that limits instruction in most residential colleges can also encourage curricular innovation. Some newer institutions have been especially imaginative in exploiting the teaching potential of the residential setting. At St. Lawrence University, where colleges are designed for freshmen, all students in each of the twelve colleges participate in an interdisciplinary, team-taught core course intended to enhance basic academic skills.[28] Sewell College at the University of Colorado and the Residential College at the University of North Carolina, Greensboro, also offer common courses to freshmen, focusing on American culture and designed to address academic skills. At the Greensboro college, which also includes sophomores, students take a full thirty hours of course work with their peers.[29]

Nearly half of the institutions responding to a questionnaire for the *Directory* stated that their colleges were begun in order to "increase the academic atmosphere" of their institutions or to "promote a liberal arts mission."[30] Despite tensions with the departmental structure, residential colleges continue to offer some of the intellectual advantages of small learning communities that meant so much to Woodrow Wilson and Alexander Meiklejohn.

Cocurricular Programming • Credit-bearing courses, however, are clearly not the only way to capitalize on those advantages. From their beginning, the residential units at Harvard and Yale have cultivated other ways of promoting common intellectual conversations. Preeminent among them has been the tradition, imported from Oxford and Cambridge, of "Master's Teas"—informal discussions with distinguished visitors, usually held in the spacious living rooms of masters' houses. A few of these units are able to offer endowed fellowships to visiting speakers: at Yale, two notable examples are the Chubb Fellowship of Timothy Dwight College, which hosts major political figures, and the Tetelman Fellowship of Jonathan Edwards College, which invites luminaries in the sciences. Cultural programming, too, has been a rich component in the life of these units, whether presented by outside professionals or by the students themselves. Former master Beekman Cannon, for example, has written an account of performing arts in Yale's Jonathan Edwards College during its first fifty years. Events, most of them presented in the college's dining hall, ranged from student productions of Gilbert and Sullivan operettas to Paul Hindemith's world premiere performance of one of his own compositions. Harvard's and Yale's units often cultivate collegiate cultural life in other ways as well, such as publishing literary magazines, hosting student art shows, and sponsoring foreign language tables. One of the more successful measures at Yale has been the Senior Seminars in which, over dinners organized by a faculty fellow, students report to their peers on senior research projects.

Lately, some of the most innovative cocurricular programming has come from newer establishments, as they demonstrate the value of smaller intellectual communities to their host universities. Sewell College at the University of Colorado has organized discussion groups around campus cultural events—including a film and a music series—that display the cultural contributions of different ethnic groups.[31] Under its director of studies Carl Trindle, Monroe Hill College of the University of Virginia has been especially innovative in this realm, introducing noncredit "short courses" or seminars on topical subjects, faculty presentations on recent research, film or video series, and excursions to art museums. In such forums, Trindle reports, students respond to the congenial setting and freedom from judgment, as compared to the more formal and potentially invidious atmosphere in regular classes.[32]

In the early 1950s, Harvard introduced a second officer into the houses, subordinate to the master, with the title of senior tutor; a decade later, Yale followed suit with the appointment of residential college deans. Normally junior members of the faculty, they brought previously centralized advising and counseling functions into the more intimate setting of the houses and colleges. With that step, Harvard and Yale recognized the value of residential systems in providing academic support services. Advising and counseling programs acquired a more human face: they were conducted or overseen by a member of the faculty with whom the students lived. In addition to advising, tutors and deans monitor students' academic progress, enforce academic regulations, grant extensions, and refer students to the array of university services at their disposal. Since their introduction, academic services in these college systems have been expanded to include, for example, academic advising programs that involve fellows of the college, in-house tutoring in writing and in science, and computer facilities.

The potential role of residential colleges in providing academic support services is by now fully apparent. Sixty percent of the programs listed in the *Directory* offer academic advisement.[33] Providing academic services, in fact, is the principal rationale for the Residential Learning Project at the University of California, Berkeley, begun in 1989. As Katie Dustin and Chris Murchison write, a systematic way of connecting students with available services through residential units can be crucial in helping students feel more at home in the university environment. Ultimately, it can aid significantly in retention.[34]

Peer Learning · Implicit in many of these goals of collegiate life is the notion that students have much to learn—sometimes, even, the most to learn—from one another. Intimate contact with peers from different backgrounds, or with different interests, talents, temperaments, experiences, and sensibilities, often is the most potent force in stretching perceptions and revealing new horizons. John Henry Newman, drawing on his own collegiate experience at Oxford, provided perhaps the most eloquent statement of that ideal nearly a century and a half ago, in *The Idea of a University*. When students come together—"keen, open-hearted, sympathetic, and observant" as they invariably are—they inevitably teach one another. "The conversation of all," he wrote, "is a series of lectures to each," and they emerge from those exchanges with new ideas, new perspectives, and new interests.[35]

Experience with residential colleges has reinforced that assumption. Reassessing the value of the colleges two decades after their founding, Yale president A. Whitney Griswold argued that students learn as much from one another as from the faculty, and "the residential collegiate unit represents the most perfect setting for this process."[36] Some of that education is academic: the enthusiasm that one student has for a field of study can help awaken the dormant interest of others; the exchange of ideas and perspectives, over time, illuminates another's pattern of thought. With the multicultural constituencies of today's universities, however, the greatest value of "peer learning" may be in the way students educate each other about their cultural backgrounds and social experience. In the intimacy of contact within the residential college, conflicts inevitably arise, sometimes exacerbated, perhaps, by cultural differences. But just as inevitably, friendships are formed that bridge those divides, and stereotypes can give way to a deeper mutual understanding. Francis Arndt illustrates the process with an anecdote about a freshman at the University of North Carolina at Greensboro, an observant Jew, explaining to his peers the meaning of Hanukkah candles.[37] It is a process that is always under way in a residential college setting, whatever the members consider their points of difference. On a personal level, students gain an emotional sympathy and resonance with the happiness and sorrows of one another; they begin to sense the ways in which particular cultural styles support the universal human effort to build a richer and more satisfying life. They begin to understand, as well, the personal trauma of social problems.

In an address at Yale in 1907—two years before he assumed the Harvard presidency and two decades before he laid plans for the house system—A. Lawrence Lowell suggested that the time might soon come "to break the undergraduate body into groups like the English colleges." At the time, his principal goal was to counter the divisiveness within the Harvard student body, its internecine separation and antagonism, sometimes along regional or social lines.[38] As newly installed president, Lowell supported the construction of freshman dormitories with dining halls, establishing precursors to the house system. Such dormitories, he argued,

> would give far greater opportunity for men from different schools and from different parts of the country to mix together and find their natural affinities unfettered by associations of early education, locality, and of wealth; and above all it would make the college more truly national in spirit.[39]

While we are unlikely to see our purposes in just the same way as Lowell, an element of his vision still rings true. Housing arrangements, of course, can be used to precisely the opposite ends; but a guiding principle in at least some of the "classic" college systems is that the membership of each unit should reflect the whole undergraduate population. In Jonathan Edwards College at Yale, for example, there are some one hundred members of the current senior class. In their homes, I have calculated, are spoken some twenty-four languages, from Spanish to Greek, from Lithuanian to Serbo-Croatian, from Tagolog to Vietnamese, from Yiddish to Urdu. The process of living together becomes, for these students, a vital education in the cultures of the nation and the world. In any residential college setting, whatever the perceived differences among students, that process of living can become a vital and especially timely exercise in learning about the other.

* * *

Ethics, citizenship, community, instruction, cocurricular programming and peer learning: these interrelated aims are ancient. Most can be traced back not only to the beginning of American higher education, but in one form or another even to the liberal arts ideals of classical antiquity. They are by no means dependent on residence. But along the way, residence has been seen as a means of enhancing them. The ideals and experience of that rich history can help to guide our own vision today, as American universities make new excursions down the Collegiate Way.

This article originally appeared in *Talking Stick*, published by the Association of College and University Housing Officers-International: 12, no. 7 (April 1995).

1 Terry B. Smith and Elizabeth Raney, *The North American Directory of Residential Colleges and Living Learning Centers* (Kirksville: Northeast Missouri State University, 1993).

2 Terry B. Smith, ed., *Gateways: Residential Colleges and the Freshman Year Experience* (Columbia: University of South Carolina Press, 1993); Charles C. Schroeder and Phyllis Mable, eds., *Realizing the Educational Potential of Residence Halls* (San Francisco: Jossey-Bass Publishers, 1994). A "Worldwide Directory of Residential Colleges" (http://collegiateway.org/colleges.html) is maintained by Robert J. O'Hara, a founder of Cornelia Strong College at the University of North Carolina-Greensboro. "The Residential Learning Communities International Clearinghouse" (http://www.bgsu.edu/colleges/clc/rlcch/) was created by Robert Midden of Bowling Green State University and David Schoem of the University of Michigan.

3 Terry B. Smith, "Integrating Living and Learning in Residential Colleges," in Schroeder and Mable, 242–44.

4 Francis Oakley, *Community of Learning: The American College and the Liberal Arts Tradition* (New York: Oxford University Press, 1992), 20.

5 See Samuel Eliot Morison, *The Founding of Harvard College* (Cambridge: Harvard University Press, 1935), 35–39.

6 Bruce Wilshire, *The Moral Collapse of the University: Professionalism, Purity, and Alienation* (Albany: State University of New York Press, 1990), 230–34.

7 Jeremiah Day, James L. Kingsley, et al., "Report on the Course of Instruction in Yale College" (New Haven: Hezekiah Howe, 1830), 9.

8 *Rice University General Announcements, 1993–94*, 119–20.

9 Frances Arndt, "Making Connections: The Mission of UNCG's Residential College," in Smith, ed., *Gateways*, 49–54.

10 Donald Kagan et al., "Report of the Committee on the Future of the Residential Colleges," Yale University (June 1984), 1.

11 Samuel Eliot Morison, *Harvard College in the Seventeenth Century* 1 (Cambridge: Harvard University Press, 1936), 83.

12 Day et al., 9.

13 Wilson, *College and State* 2: 152, cited in Laurence R. Veysey, *The Emergence of the American University* (Chicago: University of Chicago Press, 1965), 243.

14 A. Lawrence Lowell, *At War with Academic Traditions in America* (Cambridge: Harvard University Press, 1934), 28–29. I am grateful to my student Douglas Chamberlain for research on Lowell's early suggestions of the college plan.

15 Pierson, 252.

16 Smith and Raney, 48.

17 Kristine E. Dillon, "Outgrow the Place...but Not the Faculty," in Smith, ed., *Gateways*, 61.

18 As quoted in *The New York Times*, 4 September 1993.

19 Dillon, 63.

20 Ernest L. Boyer, *Campus Life: In Search of Community* (Princeton: Carnegie Foundation for the Advancement of Teaching, 1990), 63.

21 Morison, *Founding*, 37.

22 Oakley, 20–21.

23 Henry Wilkinson Bragdon, *Woodrow Wilson: The Academic Years* (Cambridge: Belknap Press, 1967), 316.

24 Alexander Meiklejohn, *The Experimental College* (New York: Harper & Brothers, 1932), 40. See also Meiklejohn's prospectus by the same title (Madison: University of Wisconsin Press, 1927).

25 Smith and Rainey, 24.

26 Smith, "Integrating," 246.

27 Smith and Rainey, 98.

28 Grant Cornwell and Richard Guarasci, "Student Life as Text: Discovering Connections, Creating Community," in Smith, ed., *Gateways*, 41-48.

29 Terri J. Macey, "Meeting the Needs of Today's Students: The Evolution of a Residential Academic Program," in ibid., 38-39; Arndt, 52-53.

30 Smith and Rainey, 85.

31 Macey, 38-39.

32 Carl Trindle, Presentation at American Association for Higher Education National Conference, Washington, D.C., March 1993.

33 Smith and Rainey, 95.

34 Katie Dustin and Chris Murchison, "You Save Our Academic Lives," in Smith, ed., *Gateways*, 65-66.

35 John Henry Newman, *The Idea of a University Defined and Illustrated* 1 (London: Basil Montgu Pickering, 1873), vi, 9.

36 Cited in Daniel Catlin, Jr., *Liberal Education at Yale: The Yale College Course of Study, 1945-1978* (Washington, D.C.: University Press of America, 1982), 152.

37 Arndt, 50.

38 Lowell, 28-29.

39 Cited in Henry Aaron Yeomans, *Abbot Lawrence Lowell: 1856-1943* (Cambridge: Harvard University Press, 1948), 169.

Part Three

ADVISING AND COUNSELING

The author, then dean of Jonathan Edwards College, at Yale Commencement, 1983

Residential College Deanships

AN ANNIVERSARY CELEBRATION

The position of residential college dean at Yale — the post that I occupied — was established in 1963 to bring the University's previously centralized advising and counseling functions directly to the students. It was intended to enhance those functions by making them available in the colleges, where the students lived. This article was written to celebrate the twenty-fifth anniversary of the founding of the deanships, and to give the general Yale community a clearer notion of the function of the position — and of the perspective that it affords on a Yale education.

OUT IN TEXAS, where I'm from, the title sounds rather august: Dean of Jonathan Edwards College at Yale University. Old Mr. Ulrich, who tends cattle at my friend's ranch near Roundtop — he, at least, is impressed. "Hayul, boy," he'll say every time I see him, "will you drank a Lone Star, or do I gotta send down to Houston for summa that there cham-*pain*?" Moving east, somewhere near the Allegheny Ridge, I figure, the title begins to lose its luster. Hit Westport, and the cognoscenti are likely to mumble some snide aside about "*junior* deanships." Cross Chapel Street, and a residential college dean finds himself in a downright fix. Older alumni, back to test their lung power at the Yale Bowl, might never have heard of the job; others, hearing of it, are sure it's a case of bloated academic bureaucracy, just one more reason why the University nearly went down the tubes in the 1960s. Faculty are convinced that the deans' sole purpose is to help shiftless students squirm out of assignments; and each new student, of course, knows they exist to bring the weighty axe of Yale's rules and regulations down squarely on his or her individual neck.

Among my scholarly mentors, my decision to accept a college deanship prompted a certain clearing of throats and raising of eyebrows, if not rolling of eyes. But in retrospect, it was one of the best decisions I've made. For as much as any position in American higher education, it puts an educator in the psychological center of the educational enterprise, where the individual psychology of students confronts the whole of their educational experience.

The residential college deanships are now a quarter century old. Initially, their presence was suggested by an ad hoc committee established to examine the Freshman Year. At that time, the early 1960s, freshmen had no affiliation with the residential colleges; they participated in a common Freshman Year program, which once had its own faculty and still had its own administration. The work of deans for undergraduates was carried on in three centers: one on the Old Campus, and others in the offices of the dean of Yale College and the dean of the School of Engineering. But just when undergraduate engineers were absorbed into Yale College, and their separate institution abolished, the Committee on the Freshman Year recommended the same for freshmen. It asked that they be assigned to residential colleges prior to entrance, and—following a suggestion by George Schrader, master of Branford—it proposed that a "junior official" be assigned to each college to advise "freshmen and upperclassmen attached to his College in both academic and non-academic matters."

In the minds of its creators, the deanship would strengthen the educational role of the colleges. The following year, a committee of the Council of Masters, chaired by Master Schrader and "augmented," as the phrase goes, by Dean William DeVane and others, worked out some details of the proposal.[1] "Decentralizing" the Yale College Dean's Office, they argued, would place counseling in its "natural matrix," the colleges, making more effective use of their resources. As chief counselor, the new official would have the support of the college's faculty fellows, and from their ranks could recruit program advisers for freshmen. The dean would oversee the academic programs of all students in the college, enforce curricular rules, and handle routine disciplinary problems. He or she would also assume the functions of an office known as assistant master, a part-time post occupied by a faculty fellow who guided some of the college's day-to-day operations.

They were enamored of their proposal, this augmented committee, but not so sanguine about prospects for implementing it. It would require funds not only for salaries, but for secretaries, office equipment, and building alterations to carve out office space. The University Treasurer, of course, didn't see the wherewithal. And as for these new deans themselves, where could they be found? The plan would require time.

Enter Whit Griswold. Yale's sixteenth president was a man of unbridled energy and boundless intellectual range. In an age of fragmenting specialization, A. Whitney Griswold spoke eloquently for general education and the liberal tradition. He understood, with subtlety, the role of community life in undergraduate education. And he had little patience for the spinning of academic wheels. On November 8, 1962, the Council of Masters met to consider the proposal for college deanships. With the Treasurer uncomfortably in tow, President Griswold strode into that meeting and galvanized it. Of course the colleges should have these deans. They should have them as soon as possible. The deans should be the best qualified people available. They needed secretaries and fully equipped offices. The funds would be found.

By the fall of 1963, the residential college deans were in place, the necessary funding generously donated by Griswold's friend and former classmate, Paul Mellon. In essence, Whit Griswold created the deanships. It was one of the last major acts of a great Yale president.

In retrospect, Griswold's decisive intervention seems especially farsighted. A recent study of the American undergraduate experience finds that faculty and administrators often are "far removed from the day-to-day lives of the students"; and it notes that, nationally, only thirty-nine percent of students report that "there are professors at my college whom I feel free to turn to for advice on personal matters." That figure, disturbingly, represents a sharp decline from the corresponding figure of twelve years earlier.[2] But at Yale, especially with the college deanships, faculty involvement with the lives of students—and professorial fonts of advice—are built into the system.

Since its founding, the residential college deanship has burgeoned. Its value has been clarified, and its role defined, by the experience of a quarter century and by the contributions of the seventy-seven men and women who by now have held the post. There is, of course, an official roster of duties. First and foremost, the deans provide academic and personal counseling to the college's students, and administer their academic programs. As counselors, they are a "front line"; but they draw on, and refer students to, the University's complex array of resources, including other faculty and administrators, and health, career, and other services. They administer the Freshman Faculty Adviser Program and supervise the freshman counselors, the seniors and graduate students who serve as resident advisers in the freshmen dormitories. They register students, monitor course schedules and changes, apply the academic regulations of Yale College, and authorize—according to faculty-approved provisions—the postponement of students' work. They keep students' placement files and write letters, and more letters, of recommendation. With the college masters, they enforce

Yale's undergraduate regulations and the community's standards of behavior. And by agreement with the master, they assist in the general administration of the college, on matters ranging from its educational programs to the allocation of housing. Outside of their own colleges, the deans have administrative responsibilities for the Yale College Dean's Office or other University agencies. And all, of course, are members of the Yale faculty, with commitments in teaching and research.

But that roster is only a dry outline of the story. A decade or so after their founding, an ad hoc committee was established to assess how the deanships were operating. "The Residential College Deans," it concluded, "are in a position to sense the feelings, concerns and moods of undergraduates to a degree that is unique in the world of higher education." That truth is the position's joy and its glory, and the source of its rewards to one who considers himself, above all, an educator.

Living in the residential college, participating fully in its community life, the dean strives to know, personally, each of the roughly four hundred students under his or her charge. That personal contact is vital, for it promotes the trust that can make the dean most effective in times of confusion or stress. Invariably, he or she soon learns, students' academic quandaries are linked to a world of other, more personal concerns. When a student is faltering in or dissatisfied with his or her studies, the dean's first priority is often to bring those deeper personal questions to the fore. The vignettes that follow are fictional — as the trust between dean and student demands — but they are drawn from my own counseling experiences.

Paula enters my office with an ostensibly simple academic query: how to arrange for a tutor, perhaps, or how to withdraw from a course. But with the simple mechanics explained, and a discussion of her difficulties in a particular course behind us, I notice a telltale moment of hesitation, a silent beat inviting a broader question. I probe — and soon we are talking of matters far more significant to her than her performance in Economics 150a. Her concentration on studies has been slipping; she's not enjoying them in the way she had last term. In both scholarly and social spheres, her self-confidence is suffering. And though Thanksgiving vacation is coming up, Paula tells me she is not going home to Virginia.

Noting a particular edge to that comment, Kleenex at hand, I press the matter. Her parents, it turns out, are separating. To retain a sense of stability, both for their sake and her own, she has presented a placid front. But in our conversation, her true feelings begin to emerge, and it is clear that on some level she is deeply shaken. The family structure and emotional support she has always known now seem fragile. With those foundations quaking, and her own self-confidence following suit, Paula has exaggerated, in her own mind, the extent of her difficulties in economics, which turn out to be quite manageable.

The conversation turning back to academics, I ask about other courses. We review her program, and a certain lilt enlivens Paula's voice as she discusses a course in Mayan archaeology. Before the family troubles burst upon her, that field had roused a sense of discovery in her, a previously dormant creativity. We talk about the need, as familiar structures and supports appear to be giving way, to draw sustenance from within, from a sense of who she is on her own. Some of that sustenance will come from feeling the force of her own creativity, both within and outside the curriculum. We talk, too, about the family connections that remain, the love that both of her parents clearly feel for her. Having been able to articulate the source of her anxieties, she regains for the moment at least a bit of equanimity about her personal travails, a bit of serenity about her less-than-perfect performance in economics, and a bit of her enthusiasm for archaeology.

In conversations such as this, deans can seldom provide a solution or a fix; but as sympathetic listeners, they can help students gain perspective on their concerns. Inevitably, they are carried into the students' world—of aspirations, ideals, pains, and enthusiasms. Their discussions with students may range over all the normal personal issues that one would expect to find among undergraduates—career goals, balancing work and social life, separating from the family, relationships with family and with peers, romantic relationships, attitudes toward religion and spirituality, and more. From time to time, of course, the questions are urgent and dire. Every experienced dean has had to intervene in cases of eating disorder or heated conflict or substance abuse or depression—the afflictions that must appear in any community of over four hundred young men and women. Those times are crucial not only to the principals, but also to a circle of affected roommates and friends. The dean's role in them is not only to see that a needy student gets proper support, but to help the affected community sort out the valuable lessons involved—about values that matter most, and about mutual support in times of crisis.

Among the most absorbing and challenging questions that the dean confronts are those that bear upon the real value of liberal learning in students' lives. Deans not only provide academic advice, but must ensure that students comply with the "Academic Regulations," the policies and procedures—now grown to a dense thirty-five pages in the undergraduate course catalogue—that govern progress toward the degree. Those tasks prompt discussions with students about the full curriculum, and about the ways in which their educational needs, as the students sense them, are met by the University's concept of a liberal, and a Yale, education.

Reeling from the death of his father, Craig, a junior, sees little value to this "academic rat race," this intense but seemingly superficial focus on concepts and classes and tests. Though his family insists that they wish him to remain in school, he is considering a leave of absence, to be at home with his mother and younger sister. We talk first of the death itself, and the way it has affected the family. The topic then turns to Craig's thoughts about the leave. I encourage him to think about the ways he has changed in two and one-half years at Yale. He came here in trepidation, he admits, wondering if his acceptance had not been some error in the admissions office. Through a course in art history, he had discovered his own visual orientation—found that he had, in fact, an exceptionally fine eye—and eventually he enrolled in the architecture major.

Art and architecture opened up a new world for him, and gave him a direction. At the same time, he took several courses in philosophy and in classical and medieval history. In philosophy, he was fascinated by his ability to follow logical abstractions, and occasionally to see arguments not accounted for in the text. Slowly, his newfound ability to recognize close reasoning encouraged him to rely more fully on his own powers of thought. Through the study of history, he had gained a sense of the variety of human culture and a new sympathy for other peoples. That, in turn, had kindled a desire to travel; prior to his father's death, he had made plans to apply for a summer traveling fellowship to Italy. Craig speaks, too, in a similar vein, of having learned much from the personal contact he has had at Yale with students from vastly different backgrounds.

But for all that, studies seem only to depress him right now. He cares little about what he is reading. The pressure, and the relentless emphasis on concepts, appear at the moment to stand in the way of his emotional needs. For now, mourning his father's death, strengthening bonds with his family, planning for his mother's and sister's future—that is where his attention needs to be. Before we finish our discussion, Craig has decided upon the leave. But I am confident that after a term, he will be back with a renewed vigor for what the University has to offer.

Most of the dean's time, of course, is spent with issues less emotionally fraught than those of Paula and Craig. Still, the more common academic concerns—choosing a course or a major, deciding how to complete the foreign language requirement, whether to venture into a new field or more deeply into a familiar one, whether to take a term abroad—all are related to students' deeper aspirations, their intuitions about who they are and how they might be fulfilled. Because of that, deans deal regularly with the very meaning, to the students, of their whole educative process. Their position provides a vantage point that is woefully absent in the highly fragmented and departmentalized universities of today—a platform from which to contemplate the whole student, the full curriculum, the entirety of community life.

The object of a university, John Henry Newman once wrote, "is the diffusion and extension of knowledge, rather than the advancement."[3] Since that good Cardinal's day, "advancement" has become a more compelling and prestigious focus, and the modern university pursues both of those not entirely compatible aims. But in our enthusiasm for advancement and research, we are prone to forget that the "diffusion" of knowledge is no simple matter of making available some learned lore. It is—especially in the open and complex university of today, proliferating with fields of inquiry—an art of communication. It is a meeting of two ideational worlds: of intellectual tradition and refined concepts on the one hand, and of the feelings, concerns, moods, and, I would add, insights of undergraduates on the other. The art of the liberal educator requires familiarity with both, and the ability, as occasion demands, to express each in terms of the other. It is in that meeting ground that the residential college dean operates, and in that art that he or she should be versed. In counseling, in mastering the University's resources, in learning the personal proclivities behind a student's academic program, in touting a student's individual virtues, in promoting the college's intellectual and community life, the dean lives with and observes closely the successes and failures of those unending efforts at communication. And now and again, he or she can promote a success that may not have been.

President Griswold's definition of the goal of liberal education is as good as any. We strive, he said, "to expand to the limit the individual's capacity—and desire—for self-education, for seeking and finding meaning, truth and enjoyment in everything he does."[4] At bottom, the dean's mission is to help ensure that that goal remains vital in the lives of Yale undergraduates. And that's a mission, I'd say, that's worth a tribute, and a toast.

For the latter purpose, as I always tell Mr. Ulrich, a Lone Star is just fine, thanks. East of the Alleghenies — and outside of the residential colleges — few, I suspect, would question the matter, perhaps not even in Connecticut Hall, where the faculty meets for its weighty and sober deliberations. But this November, when the college deans gathered to celebrate the silver anniversary of that memorable meeting of the Council of Masters, we popped open a bottle of Moët & Chandon, Brut Impérial, 1982 — as elegant a bubbly as the Chapel Wine Shop had to offer at the time. With thoughts of seniors marching at Commencements over the last quarter-century, knowing the contribution of our posts to that lengthening parade, we raised a glass to the college deanship, to its educational mission, and to the sage and vigorous spirit of A. Whitney Griswold himself.

In slightly abbreviated form, this piece appeared in the *Yale Alumni Magazine* 51, no. 3 (December 1987), under the title "Jacks-of-All-Cares: Inside a Residential College Deanship."

1 In addition to Schrader and DeVane, the committee consisted of masters Beekman Cannon of Jonathan Edwards, Archibald Foord of Calhoun, Basil Henning of Saybrook, John Nicholas of Trumbull, and Charles Walker of Berkeley, as well as Richard Carroll, associate dean of Yale College, and Harold Whiteman, dean of freshmen.

2 Ernest L. Boyer, *College: The Undergraduate Experience in America* (New York: Harper & Row, 1987), 149, 200.

3 Newman, *Preface to The Idea of a University Defined and Illustrated* (London: Basil Montgu Pickering, 1873).

4 Griswold, "President's Report, 1955–56," 10; cited in Daniel Catlin, Jr., *Liberal Education at Yale* (Washington, D.C.: University Press of America, 1982), 111.

Self and Curriculum
GROWING THROUGH A YALE EDUCATION

In Yale's curricular system of distribution and concentration, academic advice regarding the major — the concentration — is in the hands of the various academic departments. But advising regarding general education — the distribution — is administered through the residential colleges and overseen by the college deans. One of the primary tasks is to orient incoming freshmen toward some of the broader goals of liberal education. While each freshman is assigned a faculty adviser, drawn from the residential college fellows, much advice inevitably comes through the advisers who are closest to the students, their Freshman Counselors. The counselors are fellow students, normally seniors, who are selected in the colleges and live with their advisees in the freshman residences. The following talk was given to assembled freshman counselors of the various colleges as part of their orientation or training process. It attempts to articulate a philosophy of general education and to inspire the counselors for the academic aspects of their task.

LET ME ASK YOU to think back on your first impressions of Yale, when you arrived as freshmen, and even before. You may remember receiving the Blue Book, an intimidating tome of almost 500 pages, listing departments and programs, nearly 2,000 courses, and what may have seemed our impenetrable rules and regulations about taking them. Surely you had some impression of this magnificently ponderous complex of buildings, with all that they imply about tradition and power, even if what went on inside them still seemed a mystery. If you walked into an office, you may have seen a thick phone directory listing close to 9,000 employees who sustain this operation in a bewildering array of offices and subdivisions. Maybe you remember quaking, or more likely guffawing, over pompously formidable titles like "dean," and even more so, "master."

No doubt about it, we are a vast and peculiar bureaucratic apparatus, and a great deal of your task as counselors will be to help students cope with our structure, and titles, and offices, and rules. But my intention this afternoon is to focus not on all of that apparatus, but rather on what we can too easily forget is the heart of it all—or better, the spirit and the vision that animates and sustains this organization that is Yale College. I want to talk about how the freshman can connect with that spirit—even passionately—and how you can help.

Students are drawn into this social system for many reasons: it is prestigious; it holds a vague promise of a lucrative career; their parents like the idea. But if you were to distinguish the soul of this operation from the complex system built around it, you would have to look for it in a certain faith, a faith in the intrinsic and ultimately personal value of liberal education.

Now in trying to define that faith, we often falter. There is no universally accepted definition of a liberal education, no common consensus about its particular shape and goals. There is, however, a consistency in all the expressions of that faith. They assume the importance of a growing self in each of us, a core part of us that is seeking, instinctively, a larger and more profound awareness of itself and the world. They begin with a notion of the self as a growing center of awareness and see as the purpose of all this striving and activity and apparatus, the enhancing, deepening, and refining of an individual's unique view of the world.

That growth of awareness obviously is not limited to formal education. It may happen in everything we do. But the faith of liberal education implies that organized concepts are a centrally important part of it all. It implies that learning cultural traditions, gaining an overview of how knowledge is organized, gaining a facility with the process of analysis and reasoning, and with modes of expression, are vitally important components in that growth of awareness. In that process, it assumes, a student will assimilate and pass on centrally important human values, learn to evaluate arguments, make independent choices, gain a foundation for future learning, and begin to assume a role in society that will benefit both that person and the world.

One of the best statements of educational purpose to come out of Yale, to my mind, was in a report written in the 1970s. It said that the objective of a Yale education

> should be to help a student develop a central core of values, beliefs, strategies and information that is integrated and coherent enough to enable him to lead a productive and fulfilling life in an enormously disorienting universe, and at the same time sufficiently open and flexible to allow adequate opportunities for further growth and development.[1]

SELF AND CURRICULUM

Out of that, the faith assumes, will emerge a person who has a long view, a sense of long-range human strivings, of the complexities of things and connections among them, who can live a richer life and who can participate more fully, and with better judgment, in the life of the community, the nation, and the world.

Now one problem with these efforts to define liberal education is that they are very abstract. They can seem far removed from the real experience of being a student, from day to day and page to page. So to give some life to those abstractions, let me tell you the story of one student, a man by the name of Darryl Peterkin, who graduated from Yale just this past year. Like each of us, Darryl came to Yale with a core sensibility and background that were utterly unique, maybe very different from yours and mine. But his is a story of how one creative self connected with the curriculum and blossomed through it, exploring and developing that core sensibility, and gaining from the experience, as he says, "more than I'll ever understand."

Darryl came from North Carolina, a small town called Red Springs, which is racially split among whites, blacks and Native Americans. Darryl was one of the blacks. To you and me, Red Springs might seem bucolic. But Darryl speaks of it as a kind of metaphor for provincialism — a provincialism, I would argue, that in some way we all share. He called it a "closed circle" — closed, he says, intellectually, socially, and economically. Darryl is by nature what I would call, in a broad sense, religious. That is, he instinctively strives to see and feel meaning, the broadest meaning he can absorb, in life's chaos. His great-grandfather, a major figure in his life, was a Baptist minister. But most of the preaching that Darryl heard from the pulpits of Red Springs felt to him like a closed circle of inflexible rules and strictures. The circle was closed socially: few people came to live in Red Springs by choice, he says, and few left it easily. And the circle was closed economically: there wasn't much choice of work.

Darryl had a strong sense that for him, the circle had to be opened. That owed much to his mother, who encouraged him to attend the North Carolina School of Science and Mathematics in Durham. After his second year there, in a summer research program, he met a cell biologist who encouraged him to apply to Yale.

Darryl speaks openly of his fears when he first came to Yale, which he saw as a place for the very intelligent, the very wealthy, and the very white. He wasn't sure how to act, or what to say. The wide open nature of the place, the freedom of choice and behavior, so different from those closed circles in Red Springs, "scared me to death," he said. "I was in danger of closing myself off from new experiences, from experimenting." Those fears, and that danger of closing off, are important for us as counselors to remember. Darryl got through them quickly, as he found that all other freshmen he got to know, whatever their background, also felt them; and as the residential college system, humanized through the master, the dean, and especially the freshman counselor, made him feel part of the community.

With an eye on a medical career, Darryl first planned to major in biology. But in exploring the curriculum, he found that other pursuits spoke more deeply to his core sensibility. And when he wandered into a course in American religious history, he felt that closed circle he had grown up with opening wider than ever before. In history, and especially in American religious history, he found a mode of inquiry that spoke to the recesses of his own unique self. He was fascinated by the figure of Jonathan Edwards, and a professor of history set Darryl to work on the project at Yale that is editing Edwards's papers.

Now it might seem odd that a highly sociable black man could get a thrill out of transcribing the words of an eighteenth-century Puritan preacher and philosopher. But in Edwards's fiery cadences, Darryl heard echoes of the preaching of his great-grandfather, the preaching that was so much a part of his early awareness. In the words of both men he sensed an animating faith, an intimate experience of ultimate realities, which he did not share but which he nevertheless admired. To Darryl, his great-grandfather's religious fervor carried a very positive message: that one can embrace life wholeheartedly, engage the essence of it more fully, "be better than we are," as Darryl put it, "and realize ourselves as thinking beings." The study of religious history helped to distill that animating faith from the particular and sometimes rigid theological formulations in which it was often congealed back in Red Springs. By viewing religion in a social context, history showed that religion, as Darryl put it, "meant nothing without people... You can see people coming to their beliefs, and acting them out... You see one person's idea attracting others, who develop it further." All of that answered to Darryl's sociable and undogmatic nature. It implied that answers to all major questions were always incomplete, and that people could strive for better ones. It opened the circle. "My study became three dimensional," he said. "I could look at something I really cared about from many angles." And once he got involved in that, he said, "I was the happiest student I could imagine."

Other parts of the curriculum also fed into that growing vision. Darryl did not stop his study of science, and his fascination for laboratory research in biology never faded. Like that of many scientists, his fascination has a mystical edge. He sees biology as examining the fundamental matrix of life, the "creative power of the universe." And the very process of research expresses his deep-seated drive to open the circle of understanding. By its nature, research implies that knowledge is not fixed, that there are always new things to examine, new perspectives, new and more complete answers.

With that orientation, Darryl threw himself into his senior essay, which dealt with the impact of evangelical Christianity on slavery, slaveholders, and slaves in the colonial South. In some ways it carried him back to Red Springs, because in it he confronted major themes in his own past: evangelical religion, the South, his African-American heritage. It gave him a fuller understanding of African-American religions, and the religion of his great-grandfather. But beyond that, he says, "it demonstrated that I hadn't forgotten my great-grandfather, or what he tried to teach me"—namely, "that a person doesn't have to accept his situation, or to be closed to a better life."

Darryl's Yale experience was a development of that lesson taught by his great-grandfather. "I couldn't remain at Yale," he said, "without opening up to different ideas, different interpretations, and different people. I sampled the power of inquiry, of thought, of social interaction...I'm finally beginning to understand the person that I am." Darryl is now headed for graduate study at Princeton, and he sees it as a mission to encourage others in the kind of opening he gained while at Yale.

Darryl's story illustrates the animating value of a liberal education, and the core purpose of this organization that is Yale College. It is not a story about the value of a particular field, because we all meet these fields in different ways. Nor is it about a small-town boy making good. Darryl, it is true, associated the closed circle of thought in his past with a town in North Carolina. But the fact is that each of us comes from a Red Springs, a constricted frame of reference. Geographically, we might associate it with Manhattan or Palo Alto as well as with a rural town. Fundamentally, it is not a matter of geography at all. It is a stage of development. Prior to these college years, even if our background has been what is called sophisticated, we conceptualize in what later seem simplistic terms, often absolute and rigid. Early on, those intellectual rigidities are the only tool of conceptualization that we have. The universal Red Springs is not a place but an entrapment, a failure to open and enlarge that early view of the world.

But each of us, too, has the wherewithal to avoid the trap. It is not merely a matter of acquiring knowledge and skills, because we can use facts and talents to reinforce inherited rigidities. One truth, one article of faith, is at the core of my professional life as a dean, and this is it: in every student, in each freshman that walks through Phelps Gate, are not only talents to be honed, but a creative passion to be tapped. That passion may still be hidden, from its bearer as well as the rest of us. But in every one of those selves it lurks somewhere. It is aroused when their unique awareness, through experience, through encounters with people or emotions or ideas, feels itself not simply to be adding information, but to be growing from the core. It is aroused when we perceive new dimensions to central insights that are precognitive, that may go back to our great-grandfathers or to a primordial harmony that we feel with some aspect of reality. Instinctively, I believe, each of us is striving to nourish that creative passion, to grow with it.

The encounters that arouse it may come in any matrix. Some of us may have them in relationships, at the piano, or in a sunset. But the central faith of liberal education is that ideas, words, and numbers are a vitally important nourishing ground for our emergent views of the world. Our creative passion may be tapped, as Darryl's was, through the curriculum.

We are always debating what kind of curriculum might best do that. A central dilemma in American higher education today is how to reconcile the vast diversity of academic fields and individual interests on the one hand, with the need for a coherent curriculum that develops basic intellectual skills, displays the interconnectedness of knowledge, and provides some overview of human culture. Yale's own curricular philosophy focuses less on the informational content of courses than on modes of inquiry. Hence the division of the curriculum into four distributional groups: languages and literatures, humanities, social sciences, and natural sciences and mathematics. The guiding principle is that students should have a familiarity with several modes of inquiry, to gain a sense of the range of human thought, and a mastery of at least one, to gain a sense of the intricacy and complexity of any investigation. Our curriculum strives for a balance between the principles of distribution and concentration. So we have only distributional requirements and major requirements, leaving immense latitude for individual choice—and for that unique creativity to blossom or lay dormant.

So what is your role when the freshmen confront this vast latitude of choice? Freshman year can be crucial in someone's intellectual growth, and your impact on your counselees, we know, may be greater than that of any other adviser. It's immediate; it's intimate; you know them better; and moreover, you represent to them success within the Yale system. You are, as one of my colleagues put it, the "arbiters of cool."

SELF AND CURRICULUM

For that reason, your most important advice may come not through any particular information you give them, but in the attitude with which you approach the whole educational enterprise, the implicit messages you give them about why they are here. They will sense, and may absorb, your posture toward the curriculum: whether you see Yale mainly as a system to be gotten through, or as an opportunity, never to be repeated, for real growth of the mind and spirit.

We all see it as both, because it is both. You will find, I think, two not always compatible drives, or motives, in each of your freshmen: one that is focused on Yale as a social system, and one that accepts that faith in liberal education. Stated otherwise, they are achievers and they are learners. In each of them is a scared person who is trying very hard to make it, to measure up at Yale. We all know that this can be very competitive territory, in which we can become obsessed by grades, by approval, by the next step, a secure career, even by stratification, by how we stand up against everyone else according to the expectations of the system. But also in each of them is a creative self groping for ways to grow, to express itself, to realize its potential, to connect with the world, to become something fuller and better, to get and to give a richness in living.

Now the competition can be valuable. It can breed a productive tension that promotes learning. But the fear behind it can also slip into an anxiety that is detrimental to learning, because it wraps people's identity up in their sense of their standing, because it can cut people off from hearing and learning from one another, because it can take the joy out of the process, and because it can sometimes make students fearful of entering new intellectual territory, of taking on a new challenge. Darryl spoke for all freshmen when he described himself as in danger of cutting himself off from new experiences.

As I see it, your main task is to help draw out the learners in each of those achievers. It's to encourage your counselees to approach the curriculum not with fear but with zest, to encourage that creative side of them, the side that is concerned not only with achievement, grades, and career, but that wants to flower by being at Yale. Insofar as you can honestly haul it out of yourselves, you should approach the curriculum—and spark them to approach it—as an adventure that at its best promises a great deal of joy and excitement, that can help them meet the world in their own creative ways.

Your best academic advising may be in simply providing a context for the student to express what his or her deepest interests really are, to grope for them, as you ask the questions that promote that process. I think that you should always be supportive of individual *interests*, because behind those interests may lie a subtle intuition on the part of the freshmen about who they are, about where their creative passion may lie. At the same time, you may want to question their *choices,* encouraging them to think through how particular choices promote the larger goals of their liberal education—whether a particular course gives the best foundation for the future unfolding of an interest, whether parallel but still undeveloped interests may lie elsewhere, whether fear alone is causing a freshman to shy away from developing an important skill or expanding awareness in a new way.

Now one basic tool for that, Mother Yale gives you. It's in the Blue Book—three lovely pages called "Guidelines for the Distribution of Studies." Memorize that—every syllable. Chant it at sunrise all this week. Somehow internalize it and foist it on the freshmen. I have combed through many a statement on the goals of liberal education; none has expressed them in a more succinct and practical way than this. The beauty of that statement is that it expresses those goals in terms of expanding beyond our provincialisms, of expanding beyond the closed circle of thought that is our own Red Springs.

With the help of that statement, drawing on your experience and your own faith in liberal education, I am asking you to search out and engage the creative self in each of your freshmen, and to help them see the curriculum as a way it can flower. That, to my mind, is the soul of academic counseling. If you can do those things, you can really help people connect with the heart, not just the organization, of Yale College, and thereby discover and develop the best in themselves. That's an important thing to do, and I know that you'll love doing it.

This talk was published in the *Yale Alumni Magazine* 53, no. 3 (December 1988) under the title "Advice for the Advisers."

1 Robert A. Dahl et al., "Report of the Study Group on Yale College," (New Haven: Yale University, 1972), 10.

Inner Life / Yale Life

If students learn from the sharing of their lives and thoughts in the informal interactions of residential college life, more structured interactions might intensify that process. Counseling, too, may take place not only one-on-one, but in groups. For many years, my wife Ginger Clarkson (a psychotherapist by profession) and I hosted a weekly discussion group in Jonathan Edwards College. This article suggests another means of integrating the processes of living and learning in the college setting.

"MY SISTER was pregnant," said the student I'll call Albert, "and I forgot about it." We were sprawled out over the rug, the students, Ginger, and I, in the living room of the dean's apartment—or "the Deanery," as I like to call that space, in deference to the medieval origins of its Gothic architectural motifs. We sat, or lay, amid the room's dark, rich oak paneling, by its large, carved limestone fireplace, near the leaded-glass windows that look out over the leafy "greensward," or courtyard, of Jonathan Edwards College. It was, as usual, a Sunday evening, and we all sipped herbal teas and barely noticed the waft of incense that hung in the air. The occasion was a weekly discussion group that Ginger and I host: "Inner Life/Yale Life," we call it.

Albert laughed at his own exaggeration; the rest of us smiled but knew what he meant. Midterm examinations were upon us, and everyone felt the pressure of academic tasks. The pregnancy of his happily married sister was an occasion for family joy. But in the intense preoccupation with his studies and other commitments, Albert had let that and other personal matters slip out of mind. Too much so, he thought.

To some degree, Albert's dilemma seems an inevitable issue in a prestigious university so selective as Yale. This is, after all, one of the world's great concentrations of high achievers, and a place of intellectual riches and organized activities that are potentially daunting in their breadth and infinite in their demands. Those riches—2,000 term courses to choose from each year, for example—afford immeasurable opportunity, of course, making a Yale education the paramount training that it is. They promote a discovery of intellectual strengths, a honing of skills in analysis and expression, a broadening of one's view of the world, a training in the business of working in cooperation and competition with one's fellows. But a place that offers so much in those spheres—and to students who are inclined to pursue such opportunities to their utmost ability—must also take care that other avenues to mental and personal growth are not neglected along the way.

Statements of the goals and values of liberal education traditionally rely on a concept of self—a notion of a core personality, a set of perceptions and propensities, whose purview is to be broadened and deepened in the process. If that "self" is to grow in the healthiest and most effective way, it follows that the student must not only expose it to the concepts embodied in the curriculum, but also, I would argue, have a growing awareness of its inner needs and wants and drives. The student should have, in short, a growing sense of his or her own identity.

Forming that identity, in fact, may be the principal endeavor of the college years, whatever the intended purposes of the curriculum. Throughout the history of American higher education—perhaps since the founding of universities in the thirteenth century—students have pursued that end, however consciously, by banding into groups. In smaller communities, sometimes seemingly frivolous, sometimes even rebellious, students define their individual aspirations, establish their priorities, seek out their own skills, identify models for their development, and validate their sense of their own worth. Such, I'd say, is the spiritual function of the teams and clubs, the fraternities, sororities, societies, and "cliques" of university life everywhere.

Yale's residential college system appropriates that inevitable student instinct to band into communities. To a degree, it brings the student search for identity under the aegis of the University, providing it support and guidance. The residential college helps to establish a framework of values—a functional respect for one's peers, for example—within which that search proceeds. The college's authorities—masters, deans, their spouses, and faculty fellows—not only enforce certain limits for the process, but through their presence and counseling, try to assure its health and effectiveness, and to aid individual students as they come across its inevitable confusions and dilemmas.

There are, of course, myriad ways of doing that, and individual masters and deans respond to the challenge according to their own insights and interests. In my years as a college dean, I have been continually impressed by the imagination and dedication of my "magisterial" and "decanal" colleagues, as they observe and affect the social interactions in their domains. The "Inner Life/Yale Life" discussion groups have been one of our particular efforts in Jonathan Edwards. Whatever their value to the clientele, Ginger and I have found them a richly rewarding experience.

The topics for these weekly discussions are seldom set in advance: they grow instead out of pressing concerns of the participants. Conversations may touch upon the expected passages of college life, from the adjustments of freshmen as they abandon home and family for college, to the emotions and choices confronting seniors as they prepare to leave it, to the changes students feel themselves undergoing along the way. Sometimes they will be prompted by a recent event on the calendar that may carry emotional overtones: Parents' Day, for example, or Valentine's Day, or Easter and Passover, or a vacation with its reimmersion in family and roots. More often than not, the focus will be on relationships: with family and friends, with real or potential romantic interests. That focus might lead to discussions of family expectations, of relationships between the sexes (at Yale and elsewhere), of elements in the "spiritual resonance" of a friendship, of the complexities of intimacy. Occasionally, the conversation will explore the effects on the students of major life passages at home: births, marriages, divorce, and death. At other times, we may talk of strategies for coping with all of these matters: considering ways of clarifying priorities and making decisions, looking at some of the consequences of academic choices, or at what it means to "be in control," or at balancing the conflicting demands of college life, or at surmounting certain personal insecurities, or at coping with and learning from the inevitable disappointments encountered in a highly competitive environment. From time to time, the discussion may veer toward more numinous questions: how students were formed by their religious backgrounds (or the lack thereof), what now seems satisfying and unsatisfying about that, whether they see an anchor for their system of values, what place (if any) they see for the spiritual dimension in their lives.

All of these subjects for discussion, Ginger and I have found, bring forth the wisdom of the participants and spur their education of one another. In these moments of honest self-revelation, students learn of their differences and their commonalities. They learn of the values and aspirations that they share amidst their differences in temperament, personal style, academic pursuits, place of origin, and cultural heritage. They hear, and support, one another. Ginger's and my purpose is to provide some encouragement and guidance in this particular mode of values clarification, to promote an educational experience at Yale that is, in the jargon of the day, integrated and whole. If we succeed at all in that endeavor, it is because of the lively and sagacious people who have found their way to the Deanery of a Sunday evening.

On the evening that Albert made the comment about his sister, we spoke of friendships—their importance in our lives; what made them seem authentic; the nurture that they require; how, in this environment, we cultivate the best in them. If that conversation accomplished what Ginger and I hoped, it may have helped to put the pressures of midterm into perspective. It may have brought some calm and contemplativeness to an otherwise frenetic time of the year; it may have reminded us of our core concerns and values.

This much we know: before returning to the library to delve back into his physics texts, Albert, that good soul, dropped by his room to call his sister.

This piece appeared in the *Yale Parent's Newsletter* 8, no. 1 (Winter 1991).

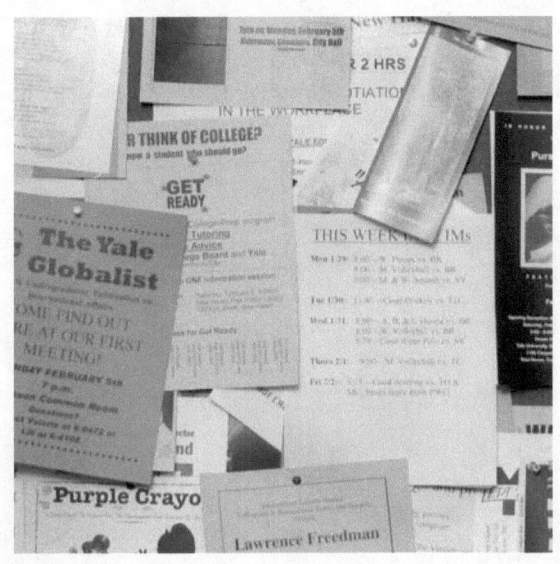

Part Four

ON COLLEGIATE VALUES:
CRITIQUES AND COMMENTARY

The College in the University

This essay, describing a tension between university and collegiate values, was sparked by a concern that institutional arrangements in any modern university tend to erode values and goals that are at the heart of the residential college ideal. For those of us who see them as primary, promoting such values and goals in debates over university priorities is a perennial endeavor. This chapter explores the inevitable discord in the dual ethos of modern Yale.

A HALF CENTURY earlier, the first seven undergraduate residential colleges had opened their gates for the first time; and in October 1983, Yale, with its penchant for high ritual, celebrated the anniversary in grand and polychromatic style. Heraldic banners of the University, Yale College, and the twelve residential colleges shimmered over the Old Campus; students and faculty paraded in academic costume; the Newberry Memorial Organ in Woolsey Hall blared "Duke Street" full-tilt on many of its 12,573 pipes; and august visitors from Oxford, Cambridge, and Harvard extolled the virtues of the residential college system. Yale University—that complex structure of a dozen different schools, some forty academic departments, and an untold number of administrative units—was paying homage to what has become the distinguishing social feature of Yale College, its oldest component. As the system passed the half-century mark, Yale very publicly touted its commitment to its residential colleges.

The colleges had been born in a nostalgic sense that as the old Yale College grew into a twentieth-century university, something of value had slipped away. In donating the funds to implement his "Quadrangle Plan," Edward Harkness hoped to recreate "the social advantages of the small Yale College of earlier generations" in the midst of the expansive modern University. Now is an apt time, as the University marks three centuries since the founding of Yale College, to review the relationship among the College, the University, and these unique institutions intended to preserve collegiate virtues in a university environment. For that relationship, with all its supportiveness and tensions, bears on the very heart of—and perhaps, in practice, even defines—the University's educational mission.

A University College · Since the days in which Harkness was formulating his plan, Yale has striven to be both college and university, to retain the advantages of each, to meld them, in fact, into a "university college." There was comfort and a grand goal in the union of those two words. Yale University could expand and proliferate its graduate and professional schools; it could hire a faculty of scholars dedicated to research and to the advancement of more and more fields of knowledge. At the same time, Yale College could continue to shape the minds and character of young leaders; it could promote the mental and moral culture essential to a good life. But as Harkness well knew, the marriage of college and university, however fruitful, has always been uneasy. Each term implies distinct purposes, institutional structure, and values. University values honor research and specialized scholarship; college values, teaching and general education. The former focus on the expansion of knowledge, the latter on its preservation. The former aim to develop fields, the latter to develop students. The two are not inevitably in conflict. But competing for resources and priority, they are frequently in tension. The ideal of the university college is a delicate balance.

The explosion of knowledge in the twentieth century, the accompanying drive toward specialization, the locus of power in academic departments, the almost exclusive focus on research as the means of professional advancement—these and other factors create a constant pressure for the balance to slide toward the university. Since the time of their founding, the residential colleges have flourished; and they more than any other factor have enabled Yale to retain old collegiate goals in a university setting. They have flourished because of the vision of their founders, the leadership of some dedicated masters, the generous support of some Yale College alumni, and the periodic attention given them by successive administrations. Above all, they have flourished because of student support: the colleges fulfill an organic need in student life, and generations of Yalies have manifested the advantages they offer. Despite that flourishing, the effort to hold the colleges and collegiate values in the forefront of university purposes is an ongoing struggle. The dissonance between university and collegiate values results in a productive tension, but a tension nevertheless, and one in which, in the modern world, the latter seldom hold the advantage.

THE COLLEGE IN THE UNIVERSITY

From College to University • Yale traveled the route from college to university fitfully, and often reluctantly. It had been the quintessential American college, the embodiment of what came to be called "the collegiate way." Founded on English precedent, that way entailed small, cohesive residential communities, self-consciously devoted to educating the whole person and focused on a classical curriculum. By the late 1820s, however, a few Americans were returning from advanced studies in Germany with university ideals. Built on German models, the university movement gained progressively more momentum, flowering in the decades after the Civil War. The movement meant various transformations: a vast expansion of student body, faculty, and fields of study; an emphasis on professional and vocational training; electives in the curriculum; the offering of advanced degrees; research as the institution's *raison d'être;* and scholarship as the criterion for faculty standing.

Yale played its role in this movement, promoting scientific study through its separate Scientific School, established in the 1850s, and granting the first American Ph.D. in 1861. But at the same time it stood staunchly for the collegiate way. For half a century the Yale College course of study remained faithful to the dictates of the Yale Report of 1828, formulated under the guidance of President Jeremiah Day, which defended the classical curriculum that elsewhere the university movement was dismantling. And President Noah Porter, who took office in 1871, made his mark with eloquently expressed reservations about the university movement. He attacked both the vocational orientation promoted by newly established Cornell and the amorphous elective system introduced at Harvard, and he preached the "powerful and salutary" effects of traditional collegiate life. But the movement was not to be held back. By 1897, when Edward Harkness graduated from Yale College, only half of his curriculum was prescribed, the other half given over to electives. The Yale student body had expanded from 601 in 1860, just prior to the Civil War, to 2,645.

Most of these changes were valuable and inevitable. The staggering expansion of knowledge witnessed in the nineteenth century had to affect the curriculum. The democratization of education, with the increased pressure it placed on enrollment, had to be accommodated. Yet universities risked losing inestimable virtues which informed the old-fashioned Report of 1828. Jeremiah Day's Yale had assumed that its main business was the students' intellectual and personal development, and it strove to fashion a curriculum and educational environment best suited to that end. The Report based its arguments for a particular course of study not on the demands of the market, nor the directions of research, nor the interests of faculty, but on human psychology as it was then understood. President Porter later defended the ideal: Yale should engender "the kind of culture which tends to perfect the man in the variety and symmetry and effectiveness of his powers, by reflection and self-knowledge, by self-control and self-expression, as contrasted with that which brings wealth or skill or fame or power."[1] The old College's main business, in short, was liberal education.

As the university movement transformed higher education, so did it alter the intellectual values of the faculty. That "small Yale College of earlier generations" was staffed not by specialists absorbed in a particular field of investigation, but by generalists devoted to the personal enrichment—theirs and their students'—of mental culture. As the Ph.D. became the requisite baptism of faculty, scholarship replaced mental culture as the faculty ideal, and research overtook teaching as their primary endeavor. But scholarly specialization did not guarantee liberal culture. Even less did it assure commitment to the student's personal development, and to a balanced course of study. Through this century, throughout American higher education, the training of faculty and the criteria for their advancement have moved ever further from those old collegiate commitments.

At Yale as elsewhere, these transformations took bureaucratic form in the growth of academic departments. Power in the old colleges rested with the president, or with the faculty as a whole. But as university faculties expanded, groupings based on scholarly interests proved administratively convenient. Initially only loose aggregations, by World War I they had become, in most universities, formal organizations—with internal structure and with interests to promote. As the elective system expanded the curriculum, and as subject majors became its focus, the crucial decisions about what should be taught, and by whom, devolved onto departments. Yale solidified this trend in the Reorganization of 1919, which made departments responsible for initiating appointments and planning finances. Since then, they rather than Yale College have determined the professional fate of faculty.

These departments were necessary adaptations to expansion, but in some ways their accumulation of power has distorted the curriculum and obscured collegiate goals. A department's chief frame of reference is its discipline; its measure of worth is its contribution to the field. By rewarding a specific scholarly competence above all else, the departmental structure displaced generalists who might be uncommonly gifted at awakening the minds of undergraduates. It ensured a faculty whose members considered themselves primarily as investigators, and only secondarily as educators. Departments may be based on rather arbitrary divisions of knowledge; but within the university, they develop competing interests—each vying for more specialists on the faculty, more students in its major, more funds in its coffers. Such interests can be reconciled only by expansion. The result can be a curriculum that from the point of view of the individual undergraduate is both bloated and intensely specialized, composed largely of fragments of learning and lacking even an effort to establish interrelatedness and coherence. The triumph of departmental structure, writes Elizabeth Coleman, has resulted in "the absence of contexts in which to think about the whole—the whole student, the whole curriculum, or the whole community."[2]

Since the Reorganization of 1919, Yale's departmental structure has grown progressively more triumphant. That original measure left room for an entirely separate freshman faculty, in which distinctions by field were minimized and fine teaching was prized above all. With such distinct values, the freshman faculty frequently clashed with departments over tenure decisions—and eventually, in 1954, it was abolished. In 1968, the faculty of Yale College merged with that of the Graduate School, a change that slighted arguments that the most advanced scholars may not necessarily be the best teachers of undergraduates. The misfortune in this history, I would argue, is that there has come to be less room for individuals whose primary mission is, precisely, "to think about the whole."

The College and the Departments · Despite these institutional pressures, Yale has certainly had its distinguished thinkers about the whole. But frequently they have found themselves in conflict with the departmental structure. Perhaps the most distinguished of them all was the dean of Yale College for twenty-five years, William Clyde DeVane. Throughout his tenure, which began in 1939, he was ever mindful of the broader goals of liberal education. As the subject majors began to determine more and more of a student's program, DeVane feared the loss of "liberal comprehensiveness" and of what he termed "the total conception." He understood, moreover, that the fragmenting pressure came in part from the departmental structure itself. In the interests of effective teaching, he fought for greater influence over faculty appointments, which by then were fully in departmental hands, and he vigorously promoted interdisciplinary programs and interdepartmental majors. His aim in supporting "divisional majors," he admitted, was "to diminish departmental control of the education of the student during his last two years, and to restore that control to the College."[3]

In 1945, asserting a need to reinvigorate liberal learning in America, DeVane and other like-minded educators at Yale passed reforms aimed at strengthening distributional requirements and at renewing emphasis on "basic studies" and "interrelationships of knowledge." At the same time, they proposed an "Experimental Program" of liberal study that would avoid "excessive specialization and balkanization of subject matter" and promote once again "the student's education, as a consistent whole."[4] With the support of President Charles Seymour, the program, soon called "Directed Studies," was introduced as a four-year curriculum; and despite insecure funding, it was highly successful in its first years. It gained the support of newly inaugurated President A. Whitney Griswold, whose own academic training—in a program known as History, the Arts and Letters—had sidestepped the departmental structure. But as educational historian Daniel Catlin writes, "the post-war trends toward departmentalization, toward the publication of research for faculty promotion, and toward increased emphasis upon graduate school instruction were none of them favorable to Directed Studies and its objectives."[5] It soon devolved into a two-year program, then later into a limited enrollment honors program for the freshman year only.

In the early 1950s, President Griswold initiated a more radical challenge to departmental authority with the appointment of a President's Committee on General Education. With Griswold's support, the Committee proposed to create a "Faculty in General Education" responsible for the instruction of freshmen and sophomores. It would be divided not into departments but into four "areas of instruction," and it would have the power to suggest appointments. The Yale Faculty, however, looked askance at such reorganization, and the plan died in faculty committees. At about the same time, the provost issued new tenure guidelines, placing virtually exclusive emphasis on research and publication, and slighting still more teaching and service.

There were, of course, some practical and programmatic reasons why some of these initiatives taken by Dean DeVane and President Griswold failed to flower. But at Yale as elsewhere, university values were in ascendancy, and even men as gifted and committed as they found it difficult to nourish the best of the old collegiate vision within the growing university structure.

The Departments and the Colleges • A parallel story of tensions can be traced with respect to the residential colleges. Yale has witnessed no more prodigious thinking about the whole student and the whole community than in the days of their founding. The makers of the residential college system created an institutional and even spiritual capital upon which the undergraduate life of Yale still thrives. They aimed to create anew organic, collegiate societies in the expanded University—societies that would nourish the personal growth of students through friendship, intellectual exchange, and civic responsibilities.

Looking back to that burst of creativity, that florescence of educational thought that placed the student at its center, we find that many of its most vital contributors stood apart from the University's departmental structure. The initial plans were laid by the donor Edward Harkness, President James Rowland Angell, the architect James Gamble Rogers, and a fellow of the Corporation, Samuel H. Fisher. They grappled over such questions as the optimal size of a residential college, its relation to subjects of instruction, the interaction of fellows and students, and the role of masters. Most significantly, they recognized that the entire system, to some degree, would conflict with departmental interests. They proposed separate endowments for the masterships and resident fellowships—"to make absolutely sure," in George Pierson's words, "that these new offices would not fall under the budgets and teaching control of Departments of Study."[6] In the early stages, the planners envisioned distinguished masters drawn from outside the faculty, appointed to unlimited terms. Masters would receive professorial rank by virtue of their masterships, and remuneration comparable to the top professorships.

Shortly thereafter, planning responsibilities were assumed by a committee consisting of the provost, the treasurer, and the first two college masters, Robert Dudley French and H. Emerson Tuttle. In French and Tuttle, President Angell skirted the departments and selected two men whose particular genius was less as scholars than as educators. A man of catholic erudition and tireless dedication, French had been an inspiring teacher on the freshman faculty. In 1929, however, he was turned down for tenure by the department of English, a decision widely viewed on campus as inimical to good teaching. Rather than move to another university, he made plans to teach at a preparatory school. But President Angell, recognizing his singular gifts as an educator, appointed him the first master—with an attendant rank of professor. It was one of Angell's most inspired appointments, for Robert French became the guiding spirit in the formation of the colleges. Master of Jonathan Edwards for nearly a quarter of a century, perpetual secretary of the Council of Masters, French took charge of planning the colleges' educational role.

By temperament and interest, Emerson Tuttle was cut from a comparable stamp. An artist with varied interests, he came to Yale from Groton School, where he had been a revered teacher of English. As master of Davenport for thirteen years, he, like French, devoted full energies to his new position and to defining the character of these remarkable new educational institutions.

The colleges of Oxford and Cambridge, which served as models for those at Yale, were nearly autonomous institutions, the centers of undergraduate instruction at their universities. From the beginning it was clear that Yale's colleges—grafted onto an existing, centralized university—would not be that. Their functions, their special character in an American educational setting, had to be newly defined. French and Tuttle were magnificent definers: with their cohorts they forged new communities, instituted rituals, molded the fellowships, promoted the colleges' cultural life, encouraged societies, teams, events, and publications. They created the traditions of college life.

French and Tuttle had a vision of what the colleges could be. Yet for all their successes in pursuing it, they soon ran into limitations—and into departmental opposition. The principal issue was the colleges' curricular role. President Angell and the early masters assumed that the colleges would have such a role: the president envisioned honors tutorials conducted by fellows, DeVane spoke of upperclass tutorials in the major, French pushed the notion of small group instruction. The educational benefits of these schemes were apparent: they would afford a particular intimacy, an especially close dialogue between instructors and students. But they would require, of course, faculty time—which meant time released from departmental assignments. French suggested that one quarter to one half of the time of the fellows, then limited to twelve per college, be bought for teaching in the colleges. In the early days the colleges did buy a portion of some fellows' time from departments; but even when paid for, the released time often did not materialize. Some departmental faculty complained vocally of the colleges' educational pretensions, and before long it was clear that released time from the departments was not forthcoming. French recognized that if the colleges were to fulfill his sense of their educational potential, they would have to be stronger in relation to the departments. If they were effectively to promote good teaching, they would require an institutional clout of their own. His conclusion, reached on a visit to the English universities, was that the colleges must not be dependent on departments for their personnel. "It grows clear, here," he wrote, "that the college system absolutely requires devices for appointment and promotion that do not exist at Yale."[7]

Even without departmental support, the colleges, through the dedication of particular masters and fellows, did help sustain some vital educational programs. The fellowship of Jonathan Edwards College kept alive the ambitious program in History, the Arts and Letters, an interdisciplinary study of the Western tradition, the last stronghold of systematic general education at Yale. Today's program of residential college seminars offers the opportunity for a definition of subject matter free from departmental constraints. But the issue of released time from departments plagued both of those programs: it helped to kill History, the Arts and Letters in 1980, and it has handed over the college seminar program almost entirely to nonfaculty instructors. In those spheres where they might conflict with departmental or university purposes, the colleges, over the years, have met firm restraints.

In association with the colleges' fiftieth anniversary, a committee chaired by Professor Donald Kagan examined the residential college system, charged by President A. Bartlett Giamatti "to consider the future of the colleges in the perspective of the next ten to fifty years." The committee's report, drafted in 1983, documented a decline in official University support for these institutions, even as student enthusiasm had made them flourish. Since the colleges' early days, the real compensation for masters had diminished significantly, as had the value of masters' funds. The executive fellows, or heads of the fellowships, were no longer compensated at all. Meal privileges for fellows, which would promote their contact with students, had been whittled down, and several fellows' suites in the colleges had been converted to student housing. "Why ought students place any value on the Fellowship," asks the Report, "when other responsible agencies of the University did not?" And the colleges, moreover, were crowded far beyond the capacities envisioned by James Gamble Rogers.

Underlying the material erosions documented by Kagan's committee is an erosion in the value placed on the colleges' central mission. Collegiate values, and with them the centrality of the educational mission, have been steadily slipping in the modern university; and Yale, for all its emphasis on liberal education and undergraduate life, is not exempt from the trend. Robert Dudley French and Emerson Tuttle contributed immeasurably toward enriching the Yale educational experience for thousands of undergraduates in the last half century. But the sad fact is that there likely would not be a permanent place for French and Tuttle in today's Yale. After all, they were not initially tenured; they did not have that requisite imprimatur of a department. They devoted their energy, their superlative talent, and their boundless dedication to the whole education of undergraduates. For all the praise that such commitments might receive in New Haven, they are no longer relevant to faculty status and promotion.

The Colleges and the University • In 1971, President Kingman Brewster appointed a "Study Group on Yale College," chaired by Professor Robert Dahl, charging it to make recommendations concerning the future of Yale College over the next twenty years. It did an astute job, taking stock of both the curriculum and the College's institutional structures, guided by a sense of the purposes of liberal education. It recognized both the decline in the status of teaching at Yale, calling for a restoration, and the excess of specialized courses, calling for a "vigorous pruning." Most ambitiously, it proposed a system of faculty "mentors," attached to the residential colleges and released from half of their departmental teaching duties, who would "guide students in the design of a meaningful course of study." The plan would have taken full educational advantage of the residential colleges.

Virtually nothing came of the Dahl Report. It was a casualty, in part, of the University's financial setbacks in that era; but it met a cold reception by faculty on other grounds. Many could not envision themselves as educational counselors; hours of advising, after all, do not boost a scholarly career. The plan promoted interdisciplinary fields of concentration, which might diminish the role of departments. "In addition," writes Catlin, "the faculty believed that the mentor system increased the influence of the residential colleges at their expense and overly catered to the academic interests of undergraduates."[8] Though the Report called for "far more systematic self-examination than has been the case in the past," it remains the last attempt to systematically examine the whole of Yale's undergraduate education.

In truth, the Dahl Report was a casualty of the decline in collegiate values in the modern university. While Yale has fended off that decline better than most, signs of it abound even here. A typical Yale College faculty meeting, where all curricular proposals must be approved, draws no more than a tenth of those eligible to attend. Teaching and service to the University play virtually no role in promotions, and the University has made only halfhearted attempts to establish a teaching evaluation system. There is no general program, agency, or center within the University that promotes the improvement of pedagogy by regular faculty. Some of the most effective and charismatic younger teachers have found their stay at Yale short-lived, and some immensely talented ones have left the profession altogether. Faculty feel no obligation to be acquainted with the full curriculum, and only a minority participate in the advising programs for freshmen. There is no institutional organ that effectively oversees the curriculum; the Course of Study Committee, composed of harried faculty who receive no released time, is kept busy approving the plethora of new courses that come before it. In all of these respects, Yale reflects wider trends evident in all of academia.

The prevailing ethos, absorbed in university values, means that the residential colleges themselves are not exploited to their full potential. Their fellowships often have difficulty attracting many of the younger faculty, who find that the fellowships' collegial ambiance and institutional loyalties are of little use in professional advancement. The mastership, moreover, has periodically shown signs of trouble. Yale continues to garner the services of dedicated and able masters, and the President's success in recruiting them has been notable in recent years. But from time to time in the past, the difficulty in persuading faculty to take the post has been an open campus secret. For all its potential value to students, for all its potential significance in defining the Yale educational experience, the mastership is largely unattractive to men and women whose primary professional pursuit has been scholarly research.

Initially, the mastership was seen as a vital and prestigious position in its own right, entitling its occupants to a professorship. The ever-growing dominance of university values, however, has undermined the post. Policy has long since required that masters be drawn from the tenured faculty, and maintaining the position's prestige in today's academic world may justify such a practice. But the members of that pool, knowing that a master's functions have little to do with their scholarly pursuits, are often likely to evade the task. The report of Kagan's committee recognized these difficulties. Its solution, however, was infused with the very university values that are the root of the problem. In essence, the committee proposed that the mastership be made more part-time, with more of its functions handed over to an administrative assistant, protecting the masters' research time. And tellingly, the committee felt obliged to call on the University community to recognize the value of the masterships. Such a recognition there should indeed be, but it will come only with greater attention to undergraduate education, with a fuller restoration of collegiate values in the delicate balance of institutional purposes.

A great value of the residential colleges is that, by their very nature, they provide institutional leverage in support of such values within the university. They reflect student needs and concerns, attend to the students' personal development, and stand for the education of the whole person. But that role needs constant nourishing in a larger academic environment that is less sympathetic to those basic and perennial educational objectives. The role merits more conscious recognition, and personnel suited to its goals. Masters should be chosen principally for their prowess as educators. The skills and temperament required by the job itself—and above all a dedication to undergraduate education, in all its broad dimensions—should be the first criteria for selection. Masterships and college deanships should be staffed with people who are knowledgeable about the content and history of the curriculum and extracurriculum, about educational issues affecting the nation generally and Yale in particular, and who are devoted to thinking about such matters. Those are the issues that might be discussed in a Council of Masters. If such criteria were fundamental, Yale might once again see a need, and create a place, for the Frenches and Tuttles of academe.

With its massive research apparatus, Yale promotes inquiry in virtually all conceivable fields of intellectual endeavor, from Akkadian cuneiform syllabary to viscoelastic behavior of solids. But the University could do better, I believe, in fostering creative thought on what we still like to think of as our principal enterprise, teaching and learning in the liberal tradition. With proper support, the residential colleges could be centers of such thought; and the first step to push them further in that direction would be the appointment of masters and residential college deans who take such considerations fully to heart.

In retrospect, the fiftieth anniversary celebrations did mark a renewal of material support for the residential colleges, particularly in relation to their social functions and their provisions of basic services. After accepting the Kagan Report, President Giamatti announced an effort to provide separate endowments for college masterships. Under his successor Benno Schmidt, faculty meal privileges in the colleges were restored, and Calhoun became the first college to undergo a complete physical renovation—the first such renovation of any college since their construction. More recently, under Richard Levin, the University has embarked upon a massive effort to renovate all of the colleges, one by one—even constructing for the purpose a temporary college, known as the "swing space," to house students of whatever college is undergoing reconstruction. The University's robust fiscal health in recent years has resulted in generous master's funds and an ample flow from other funds that support college life.

The need remains, however, to more fully exploit the colleges' educational potential. With the fiftieth anniversary, President Giamatti became an eloquent spokesman for that potential, for the colleges' capacity to, as he phrased it, "affiliate the intellectual pursuit of learning with the humane particularities of living."[9] Attempting to infuse more reality into that ideal, he encouraged the colleges to develop new courses that would be offered within their own walls, to their own students. There were some valuable results, particularly in Jonathan Edwards College, where Master Frederick L. Holmes, working with a committee of fellows, organized freshman seminars in music, poetry, and history of science, and special sections of introductory courses in English and basic sciences. The programs stimulated just the kind of interactions outside of the classroom that they were designed to promote, affecting conversations in the college, fostering interactions between students and fellows, and resulting in impromptu and planned musical performances and a lively, high-quality college literary journal. They helped to intensify a sense of intellectual community. When Giamatti left the presidency, however, such college-oriented curricular innovations collapsed for want of encouragement from above.

In October of 1983, when flags flew over the Old Campus and august figures assembled to pay homage to the residential college system, Sir John Habakkuk, Principal of Jesus College at Oxford, reminded the Yale community of the main contribution of the British colleges. The Colleges at Oxford, he said, "attract people who put pupils before publications"; they "help to insure that teaching has a measure of protection from the imperious claims of research." To speak for pupils, for teaching, for education—that is precisely the mission that Yale's colleges should be encouraged to undertake within the University. In their daily living, and especially in their personal counseling of students, masters and residential college deans encounter, intimately, the successes and failures of Yale's educational apparatus. They are in an ideal context in which to pursue thought about major educational issues, reasoning not from the needs of departments but from the needs of students. Brought to their full potential, the colleges might become centers of thought about liberal education, promoting its values within the inevitable mix and clash of purposes at a modern research university. If that were the case, Yale might build a stronger institutional context in which to think about the whole of undergraduate education, and from which to provide, for the nation, conceptual leadership in adapting the enduring values of liberal education to the modern era.

An earlier version of this essay was published in an ambitious but short-lived campus journal called *Prism: A Spectrum of Ideas* 2, no. 1 (January 1987). It has been revised and updated for inclusion in this volume.

In portraying the university movement and its historical context, I have drawn especially on two excellent books by Frederick Rudolph: *The American College and University: A History* (New York: Alfred A. Knopf, 1968) and *Curriculum: A History of the American Undergraduate Course of Study Since 1636* (San Francisco: Jossey-Bass, 1981). My account of the development of Yale's residential colleges draws on George Wilson Pierson's monumental history, *Yale: College and University, 1871–1937*, particularly volume 2, *Yale: The University College, 1921–1937* (New Haven: Yale University Press, 1955). Pierson's collection of statistics and data, *A Yale Book of Numbers: Historical Statistics of the College and University, 1701–1976* (New Haven: Yale University Press, 1983), has also been most helpful. For more recent Yale curricular history, I have made use of Daniel Catlin, Jr., *Liberal Education at Yale: The Yale College Course of Study, 1945–1978* (Washington, D.C.: The University Press of America, 1982).

1 Cited in Rudolph, *Curriculum*, 188.

2 Elizabeth Coleman, "More has not meant better in the organization of academe," *Chronicle of Higher Education* 22, no. 48 (June 1, 1981).

3 William Clyde DeVane, "Dean's Report, 1949–50," 13–14; cited in Catlin, 84.

4 George W. Pierson, "A Planned Experiment in Liberal Education," 8 April 1943; cited in Catlin, 55, 57.

5 Catlin, 68.

6 Pierson, *Yale: The University College*, 249.

7 Cited in ibid., 453.

8 Catlin, 210.

9 A. Bartlett Giamatti, "A Liberal Education and the Residential Colleges," *Yale Alumni Magazine* 46, no. 1 (October 1982): 26.

Self-Knowledge and Liberal Education

The heart of what I have called collegiate values is a concern for the students' personal as well as intellectual development. This chapter offers some rather radical suggestions for how our educational establishments might better integrate the two, and in the process, cultivate both.

COUNSELORS IN the nation's select colleges are accustomed to hearing of the "slump." In the college vernacular, the slump is a period during which a student, typically someone bright and accomplished, finds that his or her motivation for study has drained away. So regular and common are slumps that some—"sophomore slump" for instance—seem predictable crises of college life. The term tends to appear when the students can point to no major and specific cause of their failing energies: no romantic crisis, no devastating assault on the ego, no bitter experience. As the students themselves might put it, they have "just gotten turned off" by scholarly endeavors, sometimes profoundly and disruptively turned off.

Consider the instance of a junior named Louise. As her dean of students, I was acquainted with Louise's outstanding academic record. In a college full of high achievers, she had worked harder and achieved more than most, and her transcript bristled with As. But now she had come to my office to request an extension on a lengthy term paper. When I reminder her that, by our regulations, "confining illness" or a "serious family emergency" are the only legitimate grounds for such postponements, she admitted that she had no such excuse to offer. Nervously and reluctantly, Louise began to describe her overall academic situation. The term paper was only one of several tasks on which she had fallen far behind. This excellent student, obviously troubled, was now in danger of academic failure. Her conversation soon turned from the problem of coping with the term's assignments to thoughts about taking a leave of absence. Why? "I'm just not enjoying it anymore... There's so much going on here, but I just don't feel like I can put myself into it. For all the money my parents are sinking into my education, I think I should be getting more out of it. I owe them that."

Louise placed the blame for her lack of involvement squarely on herself. "Everyone" thought Professor Worth's explanations of macroeconomic theories were "just great," but she had not followed them. She then digressed into some problem of economic theory that had cropped up on a recent examination. I tried to turn the conversation back to Louise herself: to her own sense of why she had grown resistant to her role as a student, to ways in which she might characterize the psychological obstacles that had loomed up between her and her work. But I found her more articulate in discussing economics than she was in discussing Louise. Her notions of what she wanted from her education, other than good grades, the degree, and a prestigious future job, were still rudimentary. True, Louise occasionally had asked herself how studying macroeconomics, for example, was contributing to her personal growth, to her sense of "getting something out of it." But she had not pursued such questions. She conceived of her motivation primarily in terms of competing with her peers now, and of attaining professional goals later. "You get all caught up in it," she explained, "studying like crazy, worried about your grade point average, thinking everyone else is going to beat you out for a place in law school. I guess I just got burned out—like, I hit a bad slump."

Indeed she had. What Louise needed at this point, it seemed to me, was more self-knowledge—a sharpened awareness of her personal inclinations and needs, so that she could assess why she was "turned off" by her studies, and what academic or other pursuits, if any, might ignite her interests again. I suggested, tentatively, that psychological counseling as a means of self-exploration might be helpful. Initially, she reacted with dismay: "Do you think I'm going bananas?" "Not at all," I replied. "I think that your education is now at a point where it would benefit by turning inward. By learning more about yourself, you might better direct your learning of other things as well."

Louise did opt, ultimately, to try the counseling—and to take a leave of absence. She realized that in submitting totally to the competitive pressures of Ivy League academics, she had not explored the personal changes and discontents that had been stirring within, on a subliminal level, and that finally had burst to the surface, overcoming her will to play the scholar.

Unfortunately, Louise is in good company. Her slump may have been more severe than most, but many students in our more pressured institutions sometimes experience a profound aversion to long-cultivated study habits. It is time, in my opinion, that the highly selective private colleges of the Eastern seaboard, which are the focus of my firsthand observations, reexamine the ambience of pressure toward achievement that they typically cultivate. By no means does feverish studying necessarily cultivate a vibrant intellectual atmosphere. Too often, I have seen bright students take a grudging attitude toward their academic work, viewing it as a tolerable but sometimes oppressive avenue toward "success" in the world. Their intellectual labors sometimes seem to induce little joy, and little sense of self-fulfillment. Over the last two decades, reports from across the country, often sprinkled with truisms about the "pre-professional grind," have indicated that this mood—at least in sectors and from time to time—is national in scope.

What is wrong? Often, the goals of a liberal arts education are expressed in terms of "self-realization," the "broadening of perspective," and other terms implying personal growth and self-fulfillment. Historian Edmund Morgan's distribution guidelines, written for the *Yale College Programs of Study* bulletin, are a brilliantly succinct example. They promise that through the study of English and foreign languages and literatures, history, mathematics, natural sciences and social sciences, the student will achieve clarity of thought and expression, attain subtlety of mind, overcome geographical and temporal provincialism, gain insight into the foundations of modern thought, and realize "duties and problems facing everyone as a human being among other human beings." But if all of that is happening in our classrooms, the students too often reflect little cognizance of it, and too frequently seem to gain little satisfaction from it.

The problem is not that our classroom curriculum itself is misguided. But the education offered by any institution is of course far more than its curriculum. The students' education, in the broader sense, comes from a total atmosphere and environment: from their subjects of study, certainly; but also from the conscious and unconscious assumptions about values and goals held by their faculty, administrators, and peers. It is shaped by the lifestyles of visible role models, by the transactions in community life, and by countless other factors.

At our elite institutions, many of these factors sometimes breed more anxiety than satisfaction. Former Yale President Kingman Brewster, in a policy-defining letter to his committee on admissions, defined the "objectives and goals" of his University. First and foremost, he said, Yale wants its graduates "to be leaders in their generation." That is a desire shared by most of our prestigious colleges, and it is surely a laudable one; but it also has a darker side. Whatever humanistic values are taught in a class on, say, existentialist philosophy or humanistic psychology, the system in which the students find themselves projects a clear message: be a leader; scramble for success with high grades and honors; attain professional distinction. But seldom, of course, does the student believe that he or she has achieved the requisite leadership or success. Those who are taught that they must be at the very top invariably perceive these goals as ever-receding. As a consequence, they frequently doubt their own worth and ability. Chasing elusive success all the harder, they ignore other vitally important personal pursuits and leave aside even the digestion—the truly educative internalization—of their learning.

The pursuit of learning too easily becomes a pursuit of academic "achievement." In the students' minds, it can become associated with that aspect of their personality that is self-doubting and driven. It then does not seem the route toward broadened awareness and self-realization that had been promised. In fact, with its exclusive emphasis on conceptualization and "ego skills," it can appear narrowing and constraining. The relentless focus on measurable "achievements" tends to put too many students out of touch with the functioning of their own psyches. It can therefore be self-alienating; it can undermine the conscious awareness of the self that is to be "realized." For this reason, our elite colleges can sometimes undermine the very goals of a liberal education that they aim to promote.

Let us return to the emphasis on self in those definitions of the goals of liberal education. It would seem elementary that if a student is to gain "self-fulfillment" from a liberal education, he or she must, all along the way, have a growing knowledge of the self that is being fulfilled. It is precisely in that arena, I believe, that "select" higher education is at this time most lacking. The remedy I propose can be justified not only as a corrective to current problems, but also on purely educational grounds. It is essentially the remedy that I suggested for Louise. Forms of learning focused on self-awareness—including ones that we conventionally call "psychological counseling" as well as others that I would call "contemplative practices"—might now be seen to have a legitimate place in a liberal arts education.

Before discussing remedies, allow me to examine some symptoms of the problem. Data from empirical studies is spotty, faulty, and subject to various interpretations; but they indicate, at least, that considerable problems of adjustment plague the campuses. A report by Aaron Beck and Jeffrey Young in *Psychology Today* suggested that as many as 78 percent of American college students may suffer some symptoms of depression during the academic year. At any one time, the figure would include a quarter of the student population.

Forty-six percent of those with symptoms of depression have them intensely enough, by these clinicians' standards, to warrant professional help.[1]

In seeking out measurable data, such statistical projections tend to focus on extreme or clinical responses. In the past, the suicide rate among college students has been calculated at 50 to 100 percent greater than in the population at large.[2] Signs are that it climbed, with that of the rest of the college-age population, from the 1950s until the mid-1980s,[3] and that the rate of suicide attempts has since been relatively constant.[4] A 1995 survey conducted by the Center for Disease Control indicates that in the twelve months preceding the survey, 10.3 percent of college students had seriously considered suicide, 6.7 percent had made specific suicide plans, and 1.5 percent had made an attempt.[5] While the literature does not compare suicide rates at various colleges, some past studies suggest a higher one at "elite" and "top-ranked" universities.[6]

Causality in these matters, of course, is convoluted and elusive. Inevitably the college years are a vulnerable time. New students, having loosened ties with home and previous friends, have lost familiar support systems; older ones face the pressure of career choices and other life decisions; those in between are exploring romantic and other social relationships that might easily go awry. There is no way to discern to what extent these disturbing trends might be affected by controllable or unwarranted factors in the college atmosphere. Yet considering them together with the prevalence of slumps and the other less blatant symptoms of malaise in college life, I see them as further evidence that the educational process itself is often less than fulfilling.

Throughout the nation, counselors have grown concerned about a perceived rise in alcohol consumption in recent decades.[7] Numerous college presidents see alcohol abuse as the biggest problem on campus, and recent studies by the Harvard University School of Public Health classify 44 percent of college students as "binge drinkers."[8] Laws prohibiting service of alcohol to those under twenty-one seem to have done little to control drinking among college students: they simply have driven it behind closed doors. At residential colleges, they have pushed it from the common rooms to the student suites, or off campus to fraternity halls and private residences. The results may have been less than salutary. Student parties are often crowded to the point of immobility, and noisy beyond a level conducive to conversation, substantive or otherwise — hardly a setting for meaningful social contact. Too often, they seem to function as an alcoholic release from the constraints of academic pressures.

In my own observation, moreover—to cite a seemingly trivial but perhaps telling indicator—our elite students can be singularly awkward dancers. Many students, including athletes, seem largely out of touch with their own bodies, and with the subtleties of personal movement. That could be a revealing fact, indicative of various forms of self-alienation. A now well-established branch of psychology has explored relationships between body movement and states of mind, demonstrating that such detachment can evince significant denials of feeling, and with that, susceptibility to depression. A relentless pressure toward achievement focused on conceptual and verbal activities, and the future-orientation to which students are subjected, can tend to impair their awareness of the processes, intellectual, emotional, and physical, presently proceeding within their own beings. They undermine what in the Buddhist religious tradition is referred to as "mindfulness"—a full awareness of the subtleties of perception in any present moment.

One indicator of how fully students are engaging the concepts they encounter in the classroom is the conversation in the college dining halls. That is the forum, ideally, where students might share their intellectual experiences, where they might process and explore newly discovered ideas. It is the forum where ideas might be pondered, laughed at, confirmed, or rejected—where they might be related to one's own experience and intuitions. It is the forum, in short, where a liberal education might be made one's own. From time to time, all of that, in fact, does happen. But too often, meals tend to be hurried, even frenetic, taken under the shadow cast by the pressure of some academic task. Understandably, in the few moments set aside for them, students want respite from that pressure. If mealtimes are not spent in front of an open book, they often are devoted to anything that might provide a brief respite: personal gossip, campus politics, simple horsing around, but not enough of the intricacies of, and personal responses to, substantive ideas.

It is these failures of *processing* of one's learning that is the crucial matter. It is the essential reason, I believe, why students are sometimes alienated from their studies, and why the air can sometimes be dank with a sense of unpleasant tasks to be performed. The liberal education we now offer can be looked upon as essentially a honing of conceptual and verbal skills. But however finely honed, those skills, in order to be authentic—to lead toward "self-fulfillment"—must be guided by an individual's most fundamental and irreducibly personal sense of reality. In order to bring that promised subtlety of mind, freedom from provincialism, and realization of basic human problems and duties, a student's liberal education must be integrated with that "body of half-conscious, half-instinctive aversions and preferences," as John Dewey phrased it, "which determine, after all, our more deliberate intellectual enterprises."[9]

This is, of course, no new insight, but it seems to require reassertion in every generation. "The deeper he dives into his privatest, secretest presentiment," pronounced Emerson in "The American Scholar," "to his wonder he finds this is the most acceptable, most public, and universally true." Writing at the turn of the new century, William James drew a distinction between the objective and subjective parts of experience, the contents of our thoughts and the "inner state in which the thinking comes to pass." However extensive might be the content of our concepts, whatever its range over the wide world of reality, our ideas are only mental pictures of something other than ourselves, "while the inner state is our very experience itself." "As soon as we deal with private and personal phenomena as such," James asserted, "we deal with realities in the completest sense of the term." It is through that private and personal sphere, he argued, "that we become profound."[10]

In our current system, we seem to assume that this process of integrating the objective and subjective parts of our experience is more or less automatic, that it need not require our direct attention. But campus life offers abundant evidence that this is precisely where our attention should be directed. Why, for example, might a given student be attracted to Renaissance art history? Are her sensibilities more visually dominated than those of most of us? Is she especially attracted to order and balance? Does she revel in the fullness of pictorial space? And what of the historical elements: is she especially moved by the concept or movement of time, by the continuities of sensibilities carried through generations? Does Renaissance art express a certain balance of spiritual and mundane concerns that correspond to her own sensibilities? Is there some particularly private joy she takes in the discovery of a seminal moment of expression? And finally, most importantly, how do these joys and proclivities relate to her own way of life, to her significant choices, to her attractions to other people, to her other major pursuits and satisfactions—in short, to the person she feels herself to be? These are the kinds of questions that might help a student discern more fully how her studies expand her awareness, how they deepen the proclivities, outlook, and understanding that drew her to them in the first place, how they make her, as a unique individual, grow. They point to the kinds of self-perceptions that might both uncover and enhance the true value of her own liberal education. Yet it is precisely such questions and perceptions that our system not only takes for granted, but can often, at our elite institutions, directly undermine.

The exploration of such questions requires, to begin with, time. Students must be allowed time for self-reflection; they must be encouraged to experience fully their personal responses to their conceptual intake, allowed to gain some degree of "mindfulness." But our system fills up their time, packing it with conceptual intake and "achieving." As a result, liberal education can seem meaningless except in its promise of future position; it can be joyless when it seems to have little to do with the self whose satisfaction is the source of joy. A truly educative encounter, Henry James observed, will arouse "some subjective emotion." Partially through overdose, we often tend to sever our students from the source of whatever subjective emotion might be aroused. We can carry them out of touch with the self that ultimately must weigh the value of what they learn.

What is to be done? No simple scaling down of academic demands will solve the problem. Some of our more highly pressured institutions may need that, but they need more. The system itself needs a reexamination of its means of fulfilling the goals we have accepted for liberal eduction. Such a reexamination, I submit, should result in a change of emphasis. At least to some degree, our emphasis should shift from the production of leaders, and even from the honing of critical intelligence, toward the promotion of self-awareness and psychic integration.

Assessing the "spiritual problem of modern man" at the end of the 1920s, Carl Jung observed that psychic life in the twentieth century had taken an inward turn: "modern man," he said, was shifting his focus "from outward material things to his own inner processes." To Jung, that shift represented a profound change in Western culture. Scientific advances had destroyed many of the doctrines and intellectual foundations of traditional religion; but humanity still had its deep spiritual drives, and the collective Western mind, in its wisdom, was seeking to fulfill those needs with new directions in thought and perception, exploring the hitherto hidden potentials as well as compulsions of the psyche. Accompanying that shift was a new fascination with Eastern thought and spiritual traditions, which had cultivated venerable techniques for enhancing the psyche's capacity to perceive its own inner processes and expand beyond its apparent limitations.[11] Since Jung recorded those observations, the process he identified has been proceeding apace, although its farther reaches, unveiling the more spiritual potentials of consciousness, have not always found a comfortable home in mainstream academia. It has certainly produced its follies and excesses, but it has also given rise to profound insights, whether or not the universities have taken notice.

In the 1950s and 1960s, Abraham Maslow outlined his humanistic psychology, delineating a hierarchy of needs ranging from basic physical sustenance up to the development of full human potential in "peak experiences" and "self-actualization." He promoted a focus on the potentialities of the most developed human mind, reaching for what seemed its highest capacities and states of cognition.[12] To reach such capacities and states, people must overcome a culturally promoted detachment from their own sensations and emotions, integrating mind and body. This orientation spawned the "human potential" movement, giving rise to a range of psychotherapeutic practices and techniques, most of which have a common denominator: bringing into awareness one's own previously unconscious emotional and physical processes.

Late in his career, Maslow saw this "humanistic" focus as a transitional stage, leading to a "transpersonal" psychology that would emphasize still greater capacities of the psyche, its ability to encounter the transcendent.[13] Transpersonal psychology views that ability, and the genuine impulses that lay behind it, as intrinsic to human nature. Taken to sufficient depth, self-exploration naturally leads to spontaneous spiritual insight. In the hands of contemporary thinkers such as Stanislav Grof, this orientation had produced radical new views and "maps" of human consciousness that have much in common with Eastern philosophies, and that recognize trans-egoic dimensions as essential elements in human awareness and the highest modes of knowing.[14] Ken Wilber, to cite a prominent example, has outlined a "spectrum of consciousness" reaching from physical sensation through conventional intellectual processes to various stages of mystical awareness.[15]

In a parallel development, Daniel Goleman recently has made strides in redefining our definition of mental acumen, arguing that "emotional intelligence" is more important than sheer conceptual prowess in making for a rich and productive life, both professionally and personally.[16] Emotional intelligence leads to self-motivation, social skills, compassion, and altruism. It can be cultivated, and cultivation begins with self-awareness.

These various developments, and others, are part of the "inward turn" of Western culture in the twentieth century. Together, they indicate the vital importance of a more sophisticated self-awareness than our educational systems have hitherto cultivated. As the philosopher and intellectual historian Richard Tarnas writes in his brilliant synthesis of Western thought, "A developed inner life is...indispensable for cognition."[17]

All of which brings me to the propositions at hand. If a developed inner life is indispensable for cognition, then our educational establishments have a responsibility to cultivate it. For years now, some members of the medical profession have expressed reservations about the "medical" nature of what passes under the label of "psychotherapy." The very term implies that a given psyche is "diseased" and that the treatment is a medical rehabilitation. With certain pathological conditions, that is true. But the kinds of counseling pursued by many who lead "normal" lives—the various modalities that strive for "growth experience"—are, in my view as well as that of their critics in the medical profession, more properly labeled "education" than "medicine." In actual practice, the "patient" is a student who studies his or her self with trained tutors, just as he or she might study French with tutors of the language. The kind of self-knowledge attained is fully congruent with the commonly accepted goals of liberal education.

The same can be said of meditation and other practices, often considered "spiritual" and often with Eastern roots, that are intended to expand awareness by focusing first on the subtleties of subjective consciousness. Several institutions outside of the academic mainstream have made such practices integral to their programs of learning. One reads nothing of them in orthodox organs of the academic press such as *The Chronicle of Higher Education*, but in this respect they may well be more attuned to educational needs than our more established universities. Foremost among them, perhaps, is Naropa University of Boulder, Colorado, which focuses on religion, psychology and the arts, and is rooted in Buddhist educational principles.[18] The guiding ideal there is "contemplative education," which is defined, in part, as an effort to combine intellectual rigor with meditative arts and practices. The aim is to cultivate an awareness of the direct experience of learning, moment by moment—to deepen a student's perception of how he or she incorporates ideas. Such an approach brings to the learning process a dimension that it sorely needs—balancing the discipline of intellect with a radical subjectivity. Ideally, students thus learn how to look within as well as without: to honor the authority of their personal awareness, to be more conscious of their own deepest intuitions. They cultivate a direct experience of meaning, meaning beyond the literal significance of words.

Whether a product of "psychotherapy" or "meditative practices," such self-awareness should be seen as a fundamental element in education. No less than acquaintance with languages, history, or quantitative methods, it should be seen as characteristic of a liberally educated intelligence. In the functioning of our own psyches, each of us has the raw material for a study every bit as broadening as literature or the arts. To leave that material unexplored in any organized fashion would seem a glaring deficiency in the educative process.

Traditionally, apologists for the liberal arts have held that their virtue lies in the asking of fundamental questions. Since the times of Kant, and particularly since the end of the nineteenth century, the intellectual community has grown more aware that the formulation of those questions is determined by "subjective" factors, by social and individual psychology, as well as by "objective" principles, logic, and evidence. Despite the content of courses in psychology and modern philosophy, our liberal arts curriculum, in form, has not yet caught up with this fundamental insight. Much has been made of this point in the "culture wars," but the cultural warriors of the left often have a severely limited outlook on such subjective determinants, constricting them to social factors, to matters of economics, race, and perhaps gender—factors that, although they affect subjectivity, are by no means the heart of it. They remain gross, external measures of interior life; arguments based on them seldom reach into, or even are open to, the deeper interior realms.

In today's pluralistic universe, the liberally educated person must have a sophisticated grasp of his or her own personal psychology, with its personal intuitions, motives, and biases. To promote educational integrity as well as psychological welfare, each should understand his or her personal stake in the "fundamental questions." To know the modern mind, one must know one's own. Whether through the curriculum or in other ways, it is time to integrate the organized pursuit of self-knowledge into the processes of higher education.

Many who could benefit from psychological counseling, but who conceive of it as medicine, avoid taking advantage of it for fear that doing so would be admitting their own "abnormality." By the same token, meditative practices, in our academic culture, are frequently viewed as "off-beat" or "flaky"—perhaps as insufficiently conceptual. To recognize the truly educative nature of these techniques would be to erase their stigma. But more pertinently, to integrate them into the educational experience would be to further the goals of liberal education. With organized self-exploration as part of the process, students might grow more aware of how their entire college education is of benefit to them personally. They might gain a new and more joyous outlook on the value of all of their studies, and a more sophisticated means of evaluating the place of particular studies in their mental growth. In short, by being more fully in touch with themselves, they might be better able to "process" their liberal education.

An increased self-understanding, moreover, would breed collateral gains in the student's grasp of other academic fields, particularly in the arts and humanities. Most obvious would be a sharpened sensitivity to such matters as literary and dramatic characterization. But the gains in perceptivity, I believe, would extend much further, surely into such areas as philosophy and social theory. The more verbal aspects of counseling and other self-exploration techniques can surely cultivate a student's general cognitive and verbal capabilities: they demand a constant honing of concepts and refining of vocabulary, and a continuous appraisal of ideas in light of evidence that is ever-present, namely one's own feelings and behavior. They therefore scrutinize the accuracy and subtlety of expression, and help to keep it honest. Ultimately, as students discern more fully how to know what they believe—to recognize the ways a proposition relates to their ever-growing but only partially conscious experience of the way things are—they might become more acute investigators of virtually all the humanities. The objection will be raised, I expect, that such a program might encourage an excessive narcissism, a concentration on oneself to the exclusion of social issues and concern for others. But the real effect would be quite the opposite. It is largely through experiencing one's own feelings and complexities, after all, that one cultivates compassion and insight into the character and personal depths of other people.

The fact is that the college years—marked by severance from the home, by searches for identity, values, and personal commitments, and by the discovery of new ideas—are naturally a time of intense self-questioning; and the same stresses that so strongly affect the college population can, if properly handled, lead to an especially valuable period of personal and intellectual growth. Our system of higher education has failed to take full advantage of this basic reality of personal development. That failure not only has promoted the slumps we so readily accept in college life and the plight of alienated students such as Louise—it has meant a lost educational opportunity.

After her year away, Louise returned with a clearer sense of her personal priorities and, as a consequence, her academic interests. Whether or not she now saw the college experience as thoroughly fulfilling, she at least was able to "put herself into it" and enjoy some of its intellectual and other rewards. But under different circumstances, she might not have had to leave in the first place.

Perhaps I might be allowed an optimistic fantasy. At our "elite" colleges, more developed support of self-exploration might slow us down a bit—and for the better. It might modify the personality that these colleges cultivate, bolstering the students' self-images, encouraging them to answer to fewer compulsions and more genuine intellectual appetites. It would not undermine the kinds of talent we promote: rather, it would increase the chances that students cultivate talents that express their most deep-seated creative energies, and therefore that promise the greatest productivity once the initial, structured training periods have been left behind. Consequently, we would not be abandoning our commitment to the training of leaders or the honing of critical intelligence. On the contrary, perhaps we could put more faith in where our leaders might take us, and in what our critical intelligence might tell us. But above all, by increasing self-awareness, such a program might increase the potentialities in liberal education for approaching those long-promised and sometimes seemingly elusive goals of broadening, self-realization, and self-fulfillment.

An earlier version of this chapter appeared as "Doldrums in the Ivies: A Proposal for Restoring Self-Knowledge to Liberal Education," in *Change: The Magazine of Higher Learning* 12, no. 8 (November/December 1980). I have rewritten the piece, updating it in accordance both with newer data and with my own evolving thoughts.

1 Aaron T. Beck and Jeffrey E. Young, "College Blues," *Psychology Today* 12 (September 1978): 80–92.

2 The estimated annual rate has been 15 to 20 per 100,000, as against 10.9 per 100,000 in the general U.S. population. See Alan Lipschitz, *College Suicide: A Review Monograph* (New York: American Foundation for Suicide Prevention, 1990); A.J. Schwartz and L. C. Whitaker, "Suicide among College Students: Assessment, Treatment and Intervention," in *Suicide Over the Life Cycle*, ed. S. J. Blumenthal and D. J. Kupfer (Washington, D.C.: American Foundation for Suicide Prevention, 1990), 303–40; B. L. Mishara, A. H. Baker, and T. T. Mishara, "The Frequency of Suicide Attempts: A Retrospective Approach Applied to College Students," *American Journal of Psychiatry* 133 (1976): 841–44; Richard Wolfe and Sheldon Cotter, "Undergraduates Who Attempt Suicide Compared with Normal and Psychiatric Controls," *Omega* 4 (1973): 305–12; Henry B. Bruyn and Richard H. Seiden, "Student Suicide: Fact or Fancy?" *Journal of the American College Health Association* 14 (1965): 69–77; W. D. Temby, "Suicide," in *Emotional Problems of the Student*, ed. G. B. Blaine, Jr. and C. C MacArthur (New York: Appleton-Century-Crofts, 1961); and

Parrish, "Epidemiology of Suicide among College Students," *Yale Journal of Biological Medicine* 29 (1951): 585.

3 Alan Lipschitz, "College Student Suicide," at www.afsp.org/research/lipschz.htm.

4 Susan R. Furr, Marshall Jenkins, Gaye McConnell, and John Westefield, "Suicide and Depression among College Students Revisited," paper delivered at the annual convention of the American Psychiatric Association, Boston, Mass., August 1999. Online at www.newswise.com/articles/1999/10/SUICIDE.UIA.html.

5 "Youth Risk Behavior Surveillance: National College Health Risk Behavior Survey—United States, 1995," online at www.cdc.gov/nccdphp/dash/MMWRFile/ss4606.htm.

6 Richard H. Seiden, *Suicide Among Youth: A Review of the Literature, 1900–1967* (Chevy Chase, Md.: National Clearinghouse for Mental Health Information, 1969), 39, and Lipschitz, "College Student Suicide." During my two decades as a residential college dean, there were to my knowledge no term-time student suicides at Yale—a fact that I attribute, at least in part, to the close-knit communities and support system provided by the residential college system.

7 In the 1970s, some attempts to investigate empirically national trends in college drinking patterns yielded ambiguous results, but beginning at that time the perception among educators and students across the country has been that alcohol consumption and abuse have increased. See Ruth C. Engs, "Drinking Patters and Drinking Problems of College Students," *Journal of Studies on Alcohol* 38 (1977): 2144–56.

8 Henry Weschler et al., "Harvard School of Public Health College Alcohol Study," *Journal of American College Health* 48, no. 10 (March 2000): 199–210.

9 Dewey, *The Influence of Darwin on Philosophy* (New York: Henry Holt and Company, 1910), 9.

10 From *The Varieties of Religious Experience* (1902); see The Modern Library edition, 488–89.

11 See especially Chapter 10, "The Spiritual Problem of Modern Man," in *Modern Man in Search of a Soul* (New York: Harcourt Brace Jovanovich, 1933), 226–54.

12 See especially Maslow's *Toward a Psychology of Being* (New York: D. Van Nostrand Company, 1962) and *Religions, Values and Peak Experiences* (Columbus: Ohio State University Press, 1964).

13 See Maslow's preface to the second edition of *Toward a Psychology of Being* (New York: D. Van Nostrand Company, 1968), iii–iv.

14 See especially Stanislav Grof, *Beyond the Brain: Birth, Death, and Transcendence in Psychotherapy* (Albany: State University of New York Press, 1985). In this account of developments in psychological theory since Jung, I have drawn on Grof's work, especially op. cit., 176ff.

15 Ken Wilber, *The Spectrum of Consciousness* (Wheaton, Ill.: Theosophical Publishing House, 1977). Wilber has elaborated his notion in various subsequent works, particularly his monumental *Sex, Ecology, Spirituality: The Spirit of Evolution* (Boston: Shambala Publications, Inc., 1995).

16 Daniel Goleman, *Emotional Intelligence* (New York: Bantam Books, 1995).

17 Richard Tarnas, *The Passion of the Western Mind* (New York: Ballantine Books, 1991), 434.

18 Other such institutions are the California Institute of Integral Studies in San Francisco; the Pacifica Graduate Institute of Carpinteria, California; the University of Santa Monica; the Institute of Transpersonal Psychology in Palo Alto; the Graduate School for Holistic Studies at John F. Kennedy University in Orinda, California; and Atlantic University in Virginia Beach, Virginia. The accreditation of these schools by mainstream accrediting agencies, often with enthusiastic reports, is a promising development.

The Dalai Lama with the author (left) and Bernard Lytton, then master of Jonathan Edwards College, in the College's courtyard, 1991

Heart and Intellect

THE DALAI LAMA AT YALE

In 1991, Jonathan Edwards College hosted the Dalai Lama of Tibet, in a visit to Yale sponsored by the College's Tetelman Fellowship. The visit had grown out of a trip that I had taken to Dharamsala, India, home of the Dalai Lama and seat of the Tibetan government in exile. No one that I had encountered seemed to represent so fully the virtues of cultivating the "inner life," the farther reaches of those possibilities discussed in the previous chapter. So I had suggested an invitation to the Dalai Lama, in part in order to bring to Yale an embodiment and a demonstration of spiritual virtues not so strongly supported in academic life. His basic message to the students, about the need to cultivate a "good heart" along with intellectual skills, seems to me to fit very well with the concept of collegiate values focused on personal as well as intellectual development.

It is also worth noting that sponsorship by the college as opposed to the University gave a certain character to the visit. We were able to prepare the college's students, over the preceding weeks, with lectures, discussions, photographic displays, and films about Tibet, Tibetan Buddhism, and the Dalai Lama's personal story. Although the visit entailed a speech open to the entire campus and other events outside of the college, the collegiate setting also enabled some of the intimate discussions in which the Dalai Lama is at his best, and in which his extraordinary character is most evident. My discussions since that time have indicated that those more intimate encounters had a lasting impact on many of the students who attended them.

WHEN HE WALKED into the living room of the Jonathan Edwards master's house, the Ocean of Wisdom let out a hearty laugh. The room was packed with students, chosen by lot from the many who had signed up hoping to attend this event; they were dressed neatly and rose deferentially as, in his simple maroon and saffron monk's robes, the Fourteenth Dalai Lama entered through the French doors from the master's garden, accompanied by a small entourage of college officials and Tibetan attendants. In a program of events leading up to this occasion, the students had learned something of Tenzin Gyatso: they had learned of his "recognition" and training as spiritual and temporal leader of Tibet, his flight from the "Roof of the World" nine years after the Chinese invasion of 1950, his life in exile in India, his message of hope and the peaceful resolution of conflict that had earned him the Nobel Peace Prize in 1989. And they had learned something of how the occupant of the Lion Throne is viewed in his own culture, as the manifestation of Avelokiteshvara, the Bodhisattva of Compassion, a leader who neither "ascends" to his position nor is born into it, but who, as a toddler, is identified as the reincarnation of his predecessor, the latest in a line of enlightened beings who choose to aid their fellow beings on this earth rather than free themselves from the trials of mundane existence. In the Jonathan Edwards master's house, the Wish-Fulfilling Gem, to cite another of his titles, might be a presence as exotic as he was exalted—far removed, on both counts, from the American youths who clustered, expectantly and rather nervously, in front of him.

But the Dalai Lama's ready laughter has a way of knocking those barriers aside. Immediately the tension in the room lifted, as the students responded to the embracing warmth and contagious ease of the personality before them, and to His Holiness's manifest joy in their presence. Not only were they there to meet *him*, but he—as he quickly made them feel—was there to meet *them*. So that the exchange, the meeting of minds, would begin right away, His Holiness asked for questions. "Whenever I meet new people," he said, the questions allowed him "just to feel another human being." That, he implied, was the point of this audience for all concerned, himself included. "Although we meet for the first time… in spite of different appearances, background, the cultures we come from, our countries…, basically, we are the same… deep down. If we can speak, listen, on that basis…, we can easily talk to one another." Far from holding himself at a regal distance, Tenzin Gyatso asked to meet the members of his young audience as "one human being to another." How often are any of us met and received so fully—by teachers, by peers, even by intimates, much less by world leaders?

The students responded energetically, with questions that flowed easily, ranging over matters biographical, political, and spiritual. His Holiness, in turn, engaged those questions in his animated, sometimes exuberant fashion, with ruminations at once lighthearted and serious, effusive and profound. Joking about his faltering memory, he recalled impressions from the time of his recognition by the official search party, at his home in a northeastern Tibetan village, when he was not yet three years old; and he reminisced about his negotiations with Mao Tse-tung, Chou En-lai, and Jawaharlal Nehru, when he was the age of the students now before him. He remembered his early enthusiasm for the promises of communism, his growing disillusionment as he witnessed the bloody Chinese destruction of monasteries, his firm belief, even then, in the philosophy of *ahimsa,* or non-violence, espoused by Mahatma Ghandi. In response to other questions, His Holiness expounded on the implicit pluralism and relativism of his Buddhistic philosophy. He reiterated his determination to see a "healthy democratic system" in Tibet within his lifetime, and he discussed the possible futures of the institution of the Dalai Lama—whose position as head of state, under such a system, he has determined to renounce.

But the Dalai Lama's most powerful message, delivered in response to a particularly apt student query, concerned the need for compassion, or the "good heart," in daily life. The power of that message rested not simply in his words, but in his very embodiment of it, as he sat laughing with the students, in a wing-backed chair that matched the maroon of his robes. "We need human smiles," he said, flashing that engaging smile of his own, "genuine smiles." When disingenuous, smiles are repellent, but "genuine smiles bring happiness and trust." "Do you like smiles?" he joked with a nearby student. "Friendliness" is essential for human life; developing a capacity for it is essential to our own happiness. Without it, we become isolated, tense, unbalanced, even physically worn. The purpose of life, he assured his audience, was happiness. Religion, or "holiness," could promote long-term happiness, as opposed to short-term gratification; it could help produce "mental calmness." But even more fundamental than religion was human companionship and affection. Aggression not only harms the victim, it breeds tensions that ruin the mind and body of the aggressor. "Altruism, an open mind, open-heartedness—that is the real source of a happy future... Even in our own self-interest, we must treat others well." The illustration of the point was in this very gathering, this very room, where he had come to meet students as one human being to another. "This atmosphere here [is] very sincere, very open-hearted..., a very friendly atmosphere," said His Holiness, taking no credit for creating it. "So we enjoy meeting each other."

Such was the buoyant message of a head of state dispossessed, whose culture has been systematically razed, whose people have suffered trauma, decimation, and even genocide in more than forty years of Chinese Communist occupation. In his relations with the students and others that he encountered at Yale, the man once known in the West as a "god-king" turned out to be supremely democratic. And that message of compassion was the theme of his various presentations at Yale.

* * *

The audience with Jonathan Edwards students was one event in Tenzin Gyatso's very full day at Yale, on October 9. Though this was His Holiness's first trip to New Haven, his ties to the University go back to 1949, when he was a thirteen-year-old sovereign in his own land, and when Tibet was still seen in the West as a remote and isolated Shangri-La, as culturally distant as any place on earth. That year, His Holiness dispatched to Yale a complete set of the Kanjur, the Tibetan Buddhist scriptures. The "Yale Kanjur" was printed at the Dalai Lama's press in Lhasa, the Tibetan capital, from over 48,000 hand-carved wooden blocks. Its 100 loose-leaf volumes, each wrapped in the orange cloth used to cover sacred items, were packed in eighteen wooden cases covered with yak-hide. They were sent by horseback over the Himalayas to New Delhi before being shipped to New Haven, requiring a year in transit. The gift formed the core of Yale's Tibetan collection; it had been solicited by Wesley Needham, 1954 Hon., a self-taught Tibetologist who continued to oversee the collection for four decades. By the time Needham retired in 1989, it had grown into one of the most comprehensive Tibetan collections outside Asia. Its treasures—including illuminated manuscripts, blockprinted books, prints, "tanka" banner paintings, bronze images, and other religious objects—were displayed in a major exhibition at the Beinecke Rare Book and Manuscript Library early in 1991. His Holiness's day at Yale included a visit to the Beinecke, where a portion of the collection had been set up for his viewing.

The day began with a morning meeting with thirteen invited scholars, most of whom were Yale faculty, each of whom had some professional, if perhaps tangential, acquaintance with Tibetan history or Buddhism. (Their fields ranged from Sanskrit to modern Chinese history to Christian mysticism.) Ushered into Jonathan Edwards College by Master Bernard Lytton, His Holiness met the scholars in the oak-paneled, neo-Gothic confines of the college's senior common room, under the gaze of an eighteenth-century portrait of Edwards himself—the New England divine with whose mysticism the Dalai Lama, should he know of it, might feel some kinship. Responding to questions, His Holiness spoke mainly in English, relying occasionally on aid from his translator, Thubten Jinpa, a Tibetan Buddhist monk then studying Western philosophy at Cambridge University. Ringed around the edges of the room, listening to the exchange, were some thirty observers, mostly students and faculty: they included such notables as Professor Sidney Altman, who won a Nobel Prize (in chemistry) the same year as the Dalai Lama; Robert Thurman, the renowned Columbia University scholar of Tibetan Buddhism; and actor Richard Gere, who served as chairman of the Tibet House, a New York-based cultural and educational center.

After discussing the suppression of religion in Tibet, and such basic Buddhist concepts as the nature of the self and of afterlife, the Dalai Lama turned to questions regarding the relationship of Buddhism to the Western intellectual tradition. The interaction between East and West, in his view, results in unpredictable but fruitful hybrids. As Buddhism varies in its differing cultural milieus across Asia, so any Buddhist practice in the West must incorporate Western elements. While the most basic truths do not need to vary, the emphases inevitably do. Asked what aspects of American culture are most appealing to Buddhists, His Holiness praised the traditions of skepticism and empiricism in Western intellectual life, the renouncing of foregone conclusions, the demand for evidence. Those trends accord with an important strain in the thought of the Buddha himself, who asked that his tenets be accepted only if they proved true in a follower's own experience, and they make for a lively and inquisitive intellectual life. "When I explain Buddhism to my own people, I sometimes feel boring," he laughed; "but Americans, they ask questions and take notes!"

It was no bored group that listened to His Holiness that morning, as he responded to questions on such matters as the cause and purpose of suffering, and the starting point in spiritual practice. The strongest reactions, once again, were to Tenzin Gyatso's presence, even more than to his words. "I found it extraordinarily energizing to my own sense of imagination as a Christian," said the Rev. Katherine Latimer, associate pastor of the Church of Christ in Yale. Seeing that "incredibly centered person" interacting with his interpreter, in their fond relationship of teacher and disciple, and seeing him interact with the others there, fully as aware of the observers on the periphery of the room as of the intellectual luminaries around the central table—"that allowed me," she said, "to picture Jesus as a human being, to imagine how He may have been witnessed by those who saw Him."

The Rev. Latimer was particularly taken by the Dalai Lama's response to a question put by Rabbi James Ponet, Yale's Jewish chaplain, on the purpose of suffering. Although His Holiness alluded to the Buddhist notion of karma, both Latimer and Ponet heard echoes of their own religious traditions. The concept of karma emphasizes one's own role in creating his or her situation, as well as the opportunities that situation affords for spiritual growth; and it highlights the futility of simply blaming others for one's travails. "I come back to what he said a lot, I reflect on it," Ponet said later; "if we face that suffering and go through it, we can reach new levels of purity." Ponet took particular note of a reference to Tibetan monks who had spent years in prison, and who later reported that they found their happiest moments there, because of the mental state they were able to cultivate in the process. "I felt enormously lightened when I left," he commented; "I heard my own tradition more clearly." He heard that tradition especially in the Dalai Lama's closing comments, in answer to a question about how one could best begin spiritual practice. The most important element, said His Holiness, is "a good heart"—toward oneself, toward others, toward the world. For the Rabbi, His Holiness's words echoed the Ethics of the Fathers, a third-century work included in the Talmud. The Dalai Lama's teaching was simple: whether or not one has religion, a "good heart" creates good interactions—with one's self, with others, with the environment. Coming from Tenzin Gyatso, that simple message—which in other contexts could sound trite or naive—came across to many with a profound credibility. "Just by being in his presence," said Jael Kampfe, one of the students in attendance, "you know that he embodies what he's saying—that's the incredible thing."

* * *

All of that emphasis on the good heart and the spiritual quest does not exclude the Dalai Lama from the realm of Caesar. He remains the political leader of his people: the foremost international advocate for a Tibet free of Chinese domination; the chief executive for the progressively more organized, if scattered, Tibetan community in exile; a guiding force in the creation of a new polity, a new democratic constitution, for a future Tibetan state. He arrived at Yale on the heels of a trip to the newly liberated Baltic states and a newly de-communized Bulgaria. Events in eastern Europe in the previous two years, and particularly in the Baltics, had injected new hope into the Tibetan cause. "Just as the people of the Baltic States have been successful in regaining their freedom," said the Dalai Lama in a statement prepared for his Yale press conference, "I am confident that we Tibetans will soon regain ours." His Holiness chose New Haven as the place to make a major public announcement: that after more than three decades in exile, he would press Chinese authorities to permit him to visit

Tibet—in the company of Chinese officials, "many of my friends who will be keen to accompany me," and representatives of the international media. That announcement set the agenda for the press conference and dominated coverage of the Dalai Lama's appearance at Yale in the national press.

His Holiness gave two reasons for wishing such a visit: to educate the Chinese regarding the "true feelings" of the Tibetan people about the Chinese occupation, and to ward off a violent Tibetan response to recent Chinese repressions. In truth, however, neither the Dalai Lama nor members of his government in exile realistically could have had much hope for a positive Chinese response. The Chinese government had suggested a return to Tibet before, but only under restrictive terms that the Tibetans considered unacceptable and threatening to the Dalai Lama's personal security and freedom. In proposing a visit that would allow him to meet freely with the Tibetan people, under the gaze of the international press, the Dalai Lama was at least keeping international attention on the Tibetan situation.

That situation has certainly given the Tibetan people cause to know suffering. In 1960, the International Commission of Jurists labeled Chinese actions in Tibet a genocide. Western and Tibetan sources estimate that 1.2 million people—a sixth of the Tibetan population—have died as a result of the Chinese occupation, through executions, starvation, imprisonment and suicide. Over six thousand monasteries, many in existence for centuries, have been razed, and their precious religious artifacts destroyed or sold. There have been widespread reports of political imprisonment, torture, mandatory sterilization, and forced abortions. The Tibetan ecology has been severely disrupted with deforestation, extermination of wildlife, and the dumping of nuclear waste. Three to five hundred thousand Chinese troops—and a quarter of China's nuclear missile force—are stationed in Tibet. A policy of population transfer has brought more than seven million Chinese into the country, making the native Tibetans—with their distinct language, culture, and religion—a minority in their own land. Segregation and open discrimination—in education, medical care, employment, and political control—make the country a rigidly two-tiered society.

Such extremes of repression could lead easily to dispirited capitulation or desperate guerrilla warfare. Guided by his Buddhist principles, however, the Dalai Lama has steered a radically different course. While resolutely asserting the Tibetan national identity, and building institutions outside of the country to assure its survival, he has consistently discouraged a violent nationalism. In response to Chinese violations of human rights, he has called for international diplomatic and economic sanctions. At the same time, he has recognized that, in the long term, the Chinese—one quarter of the human population, he frequently reminds his audience—cannot remain isolated from the world community, and he expects the eventual triumph of democratic reforms. Above all he has been careful, despite the traumas visited on his own people, to discourage ethnic or nationalistic hatreds.

At the heart of his political position is a spiritual stance, an identification with a common humanity. A telling moment came at the press conference, which was devoted to political concerns and the suggested visit to Tibet. How, the Dalai Lama was asked, did he feel, personally, about returning to his homeland after more than thirty years of enforced exile? The answer was surprising. On an "emotional level, I think, not much," he responded. "I always consider the whole [of] this world [as the] same home of humanity. I consider myself a citizen of the world, one of the human beings on this planet. So wherever you receive some human smiles, some human affection, I consider this more important, even though [in] my own country, because of the situation, [there has been] so much tension, so much suffering, so much terror." At a luncheon honoring His Holiness, held in the circular, elegant Presidents' Room of Woolsey Hall, President Benno Schmidt summed up the Dalai Lama's political contribution on the world stage. "His Holiness has spoken with great eloquence," said Schmidt, "of the sense of universal responsibility at the core of human and political relations. That is an essential, ecumenical view of ourselves, at the heart of the struggle for human rights, political pluralism, and civic virtue."

* * *

The underpinnings of that sense of universal responsibility were the subject of the Dalai Lama's public address, held in the late afternoon at the beautifully restored—and fully packed—Battell Chapel, a Victorian Gothic setting glistening with stenciled gray, green, and maroon wall decoration, carved wooden paneling, gold edging, and stained glass. The general subject and publicized title, "Facing the Enemy," had been chosen at Yale, with a cognizance of His Holiness's philosophy in these matters. By the time he arrived, however, His Holiness had altered the title in a way that took the concept a step further: he came with a prepared text entitled "Embracing the Enemy." Although the text addressed Buddhist notions of compassion toward an adversary, much of it focused on the proposed visit to Tibet. During the day, however, His Holiness sensed that the moment called for a fuller exploration of the philosophical and spiritual side of his subject. By the time he arrived at Battell, having already spoken extensively of the proposed trip at the press conference, he had determined to depart from his prepared text. Introduced by Master Lytton as "the conscience of science," he spoke *ex tempore*—predominantly in English, occasionally through his translator.

The philosophical starting point for the Dalai Lama's approach to conflict and to world affairs is a sense of a common, and fundamentally compassionate, human nature. All human beings, he argued, are basically the same. They want happiness and freedom from suffering. The very foundation of this shared human life is human affection: conception results from love between parents; and the physical as well as emotional nourishment of the infant depends on affection between the child and mother, on nursing and touch. We are social animals: without companionship, we cannot survive. Human life requires affection. The prevalence of violence give us an impression that human nature is aggressive, but if aggressiveness really dominated over affection, the world would not face a problem of overpopulation. Most of us are involved in compassionate acts—in taking care of children and of others, in promoting life. "I believe, basically, human nature is gentleness," said His Holiness, "human nature is compassionate, not aggressive."

If we examine our basic nature, it becomes possible to increase the force of compassion in our lives. The concept that human beings are fundamentally the same is crucial: if we acknowledge it, then we can more easily resolve conflicts between groups and between individuals. The distinctions we make among ourselves, dividing the world into "us" and "them," are artificial and manmade: to some extent, they are departures from our more fundamental natures. Children, observed His Holiness, can live and play happily together, despite national differences and even hostilities. A learned "sophistication" in our thinking, for all of its virtues, can create "conceptual troubles" and "barriers to communication at the most human level." "Human intelligence...[is] very good, wonderful. However, that intelligence, balanced by a good heart...becomes more constructive. Without proper balance by a good heart, then sometimes human intelligence creates unhappy events."

Problems that the world is facing today—with the environment, for example, and the international economy—are global problems, beyond the capacities of single nations to solve on their own. Their solutions require a sense of universal responsibility, based on compassion. The obstacles to such compassion are hatred and jealousy, usually directed against an "external enemy." But the greater enemy, said His Holiness, is internal, in the form of hatred and jealousy itself. By definition, the enemy is someone or something that destroys happiness, or the source of happiness. While an external enemy, another human being, can destroy secondary sources of happiness, such as wealth, fame, and friendships, he or she cannot destroy the "substantial" source of happiness, which is "mental calmness." Inner enemies such as hatred, however, attack the mental equilibrium of the one who hates. Former external enemies, once relieved of their own hatred, can become friends; but hatred itself is always destructive. When we face a tragedy or misfortune, we inevitably feel anger. But anger produces "blind energy": while it can be constructive, it often is destructive and often gets in the way of a "clear realization," a clear analysis, of the situation. "Inner strength" is better promoted by patience, tolerance, and respect for the external adversary. Those qualities do not imply acquiescence; they allow for "strong countermeasures" against aggression, countermeasures made more effective by judgment unclouded by anger. In his own case, said the Dalai Lama, his most difficult period turned out to be in some ways his best, training him to develop determination, cultivating his inner strength. The external enemy, then, can be seen and even appreciated as a useful teacher, one who teaches the value of patience and tolerance.

Answering the questions that followed his talk, His Holiness provided a glimpse of some of the meditational practices that support his philosophy. One of his exercises, a practice known as "giving and taking," entails visualizing the Chinese guards who have brutalized his countrymen. From that image of "the enemy," he visualizes the "taking away" of the traits that motivate their violence: their own ignorance, anger, hatred, and suffering. And toward that image he visualizes the coming, the "giving," of compassion, love, and good fortune. Through such practices, the Dalai Lama develops his own compassion for the "enemy." As compassion develops, fear is reduced, he argued, and doors to communication are opened. We come to avoid acts, such as acts of violent retaliation, that simply bring more suffering. Asked whether he did not feel anger himself, His Holiness acknowledged that he did, certainly upon hearing of repressions in his homeland. But anger itself is temporary and impulsive; the goal is to feel anger, when feel it we must, without hatred. In response to a question of how he dealt with sorrow, His Holiness turned to the Buddhist notion that any event has many aspects, good as well as bad. If a tragedy has already occurred, worry is of little use. Better to accept the past event and be aware of the value that has come out of it. In that way, the apparent enormity of the loss subsides. As leader of the Tibetans, for example, the Dalai Lama has lost his country. But in the process, he reported, he has been liberated from the traditional constraints that a royal life in Lhasa, the Tibetan capital, would have imposed. He has gained the opportunity to meet other people and to know other cultures.

He has also come to know other religions. From the Dalai Lama's point of view, the greatest tragedy is for religion itself to become a source of conflict, to undermine the sense of universal responsibility. Ensconced in Lhasa as a youth, he had assumed the superiority of Buddhism. But contact with spiritual striving throughout the globe has shown him, he told his audience, that all major world religions have the same potential to produce better human beings, people who are dedicated, "warm-hearted," compassionate, and good. Despite their philosophical differences, all teach the same fundamental ethics: they teach love, compassion, and forgiveness. Each of them can learn from the traditions and practices of the others, and harmony among them is essential.

In his closing message to the students in his audience, the Dalai Lama returned to the theme that he considers even more fundamental than religion: the good heart. "Learning, increasing human intelligence or human knowledge, is very essential, very important." he told them. "However, that alone [is] not [the] full answer for your life... Education [is] something like an instrument. Whether that instrument [is] used properly or not, effectively or not..., whether it becomes constructive or destructive, depends on your own heart. So therefore, while you [are] gaining new knowledge day by day, it is equally important to take care about your good heart."

* * *

At the close of the Dalai Lama's address, Charles Krigbaum, Professor of Music and University Organist, produced out of the Battell Chapel organ the haunting sounds of the Tibetan national anthem. It was the second time during the day that His Holiness, to his surprise, had heard those strains—so exotic to Western ears, with their steady, bass drone accompanied by an ethereal melody reaching into some of the highest ranges on the instrument. Earlier, at the luncheon in the Presidents' Room, the instrument was human voices. Into the room filed the Whiffenpoofs of 1992, singing "Aj Lucka Lucka," their traditional entrance song, followed by a particularly soulful arrangement of "the Whiffenpoof Song," their traditional closing number. But instead of marching out of the room after intoning of the tables down at Mory's, the "gentleman songsters" took up the rumbling drone of the anthem, singing the Tibetan lyrics to the melody.

The surprise performance had been conceived by Manoel Felciano, a Whiffenpoof who was working in the Jonathan Edwards College master's office, and Barbara Goddard, senior administrative assistant to the master. Calling the Office of Tibet in New York to request the anthem's lyrics, Ms. Goddard was met by a bemused skepticism. The lyrics were in Tibetan: how could the students sing them? "This is *Yale*," she replied. "They'll *learn* them." As Felciano acknowledged later, mastering neither the lyrics (by phonetic transcription) nor the music was easy. "Our basses barely reached those low notes," he said, "and the melody has an uncommonly large range—two octaves—reaching very high. It was very different from any Western tonality we were used to." The difficulty was not lost on Tenzin Gyatso, who was visibly moved by the performance. After the meal, draped in the blue and white Yale scarf presented to him by Master Lytton, he expressed his appreciation. But again, it was his presence even more than the content of his words that made the moment. As the Whiffenpoofs moved to file out of the room, expecting to disappear as they normally do after performances before dignitaries, His Holiness left his place at the head table and hastened over to the doorway to meet them. One by one he greeted them and thanked them for their gesture—as one human being to another. "We were all surprised, and very touched, by the way he received us," said Felciano. "Everybody had an ear-to-ear smile."

That was just one more way in which the Ocean of Wisdom, in his day at Yale, spread those genuine smiles that he considers so essential to developing the good heart. "He diffused tension wherever he went," reported Felciano, who attended several of the day's events. "He possesses a kind of warmth and kindness that is so genuine. As soon as people met him, they completely relaxed." For Felciano, the visit was "a sea of tranquility in the rough waters of Yale." In a high-powered academic institution like ours, he explained, there's "so much pressure, stress, anxiety. People take that for granted until someone like the Dalai Lama comes along and shows you what it is to be at peace with yourself."

This article was published, in slightly abbreviated form, in a campus journal entitled *International Forum at Yale* 12, no. 1 (Spring 1992).

Coda

Why J.E. Sux

THE SPIRIT OF A RESIDENTIAL COLLEGE

Each year since it opened in 1933, Jonathan Edwards College has celebrated the birthday of its eponym with a feast. These dinners normally have included a talk or presentation on Edwards himself. In my last semester as dean, I was invited to give the talk, which became, in effect, a valedictory.

ON THIS SOLEMN occasion, we celebrate both Jonathan Edwards College and the man whose name it bears, and I hope that you will allow me a few words about the heart and soul of each. Regarding the college, the most profound question we could ask—the query of queries—is of course, this: "Why does J.E. suck?" There is both an historical and an ontological answer to that question. Allow me to address them both.

For those among you who might not be aware of it, I should explain that the cry of "J.E. Sux"—spelled *s-u-x*—despite its seeming self-deprecation is, in fact, a rallying cry of pride, the clarion that this past year trumpeted the college to its first intramural athletic championship since 1959. I have a special vantage point on this query of queries, since J.E. began to suck precisely on November 1, 1975, only a few months before I became dean. The time in which J.E. has sucked, therefore, corresponds almost exactly to the period of my deanship. Not that I bear any responsibility for it, mind you, since on that fateful day in 1975 I was serving safely as acting dean of Calhoun College. But I do consider it my grave moral obligation to address this question, especially as historian, since that is my profession and since after my departure, I don't know that there will be anyone around to tell the story.

In Mexico in 1975, that particular weekend meant the Day of the Dead; elsewhere in America, it meant All Hallow's Eve; but at Yale it meant... BLADDERBALL! Bladderball was the annual ritual unique to this campus, timed generally for the Saturday morning of Dartmouth Weekend, just after midterm, when spirits were most in need of venting. Each of the colleges and major extracurricular organizations formed teams, or better said, mobs; they gathered on the Old Campus, squawked at, rushed at, and insulted one another—until without warning an inflated canvas ball six feet in diameter rolled from Phelps Gate into the crowd. Whichever team could get this monstrous sphere out of the Old Campus, normally over the High Street fence, was declared the winner; the ball was then borne up Hillhouse Avenue and ceremoniously turned over to the President at his house.

To understand the dynamics of that memorable November 1, you have to appreciate the pitch of excitement that rose to a crescendo in anticipation of the day. As a broadside in the *Yale Daily News* put it two days earlier, "In the future, wars will not exist—but there will be... Bladderball!" Teams issued threats and insults in the *News*, which organized the event. That year, for example, Davenport declared, "You wanna die? Meet us at 10 and bring an ID so we can notify your next-of-kin." The *News* countered—with uncharacteristic accuracy—that the Oldest College Daily "leads the nation in total offensiveness." Everyone claimed an unbroken string of victories in the past, and WYBC, the University radio station, thanked the "participants who year after year willingly cast their bodies beneath our heels, squirming and kicking like spiders on a hot stove."

That tasteless denigration of spiders, our college mascot, could not have gone down well in J.E.; and here a small group of seniors hatched an ingenious plot. A few of them would hide out in an upper-floor room of McClellan Hall with a rope attached to a grappling hook. When the ball was released, some of their co-conspirators on the field would maneuver it into position and attach the hook; it would then be whisked up above the crowd and tossed to other, waiting members of the team, who would spirit it over the fence.

Initially, the plan worked gorgeously: the J.E. team on the field got the ball into position just moments after it hit the Old Campus. But alas, the hook punctured the ball; it quickly deflated just after it had rolled through Phelps Gate; and Bladderball '75 came to an abrupt, ignominious, and anti-climactic end. Other teams got a sense of who was responsible, and though the conspirators managed to escape with their lives, cries of "J.E. sucks" broke out on the Old Campus. The *Daily News* later recorded the aftermath, which was well worthy of the Day of the Dead:

> After the Bladderball's untimely demise, mourners carried its limp remains to CCL, around the circulation desk, and tried to put it on closed reserve. The grief-

crazed Ballbearers then dragged it up Hillhouse and presented it to the President. Brewster led a death chant ("give me a 'B,'" etc.) and threw the crowd a volleyball in return.

Later at the Yale Bowl, during the Dartmouth Game, in the midst of an uninspiring cheer that was falling flat, a lone voice warbled "J.E. sucks." That solitary cry, however, was the voice of fate, for it tapped the disappointment of the crowd. Soon the entire Yale student section—or eleven-twelfths of it—was erupting with the chant, "J.E. sucks!"

The words stuck, even if their bitter edge began to soften. They were taken up regularly at subsequent football games; and in the spring, when it was announced in Calhoun College that their acting dean would become dean of J.E., I was met with good-natured cries in the dining hall and courtyard of "J.E. sucks." And I wondered, my God, what had I taken on.

Men and women of the college, I bring you to the nadir of J.E.'s reputation. It is, however, testimony to the indomitable spirit of this college that before long the taunt became a rallying cry, the term of opprobrium a badge of honor. Credit for that belongs especially to one group—the magnificent J.E. hockey team of the 1976-77 year, which began to call itself the "Sux," spelled *s-u-x*. At a time when the college stood near the bottom of intramural Tyng Cup rankings, it was hard to argue with the performance of the J.E. Sux. They rolled over Davenport, bashed Timothy Dwight, crushed Calhoun; and the college rallied behind them, turning out in crowds for late-night games at Ingalls Rink, chanting with exuberance and renewed pride, "J.E. Sux!"

Inspired by that chant, the team rolled on undefeated—not only that year, but for the next three years to come. They broke the record for the longest undefeated streak in the history of Yale intramural sports and then kept on winning, forging a new record of 55 games that still gloriously stands. They had cheerleaders; they had a student begin games by singing the national anthem; and the Yale hockey coach was heard to remark that he wished *his* team could bring out crowds like that. They won four straight championships—and it was all to the chant of "J.E. Sux!" The inevitable tee-shirts appeared in the college, saying "Sux et Veritas." The moniker "Sux" spread to other J.E. teams and then became a rallying cry for the college as a whole, as it has been right up until now, in days of even greater glory, when we could do the unthinkable and capture the Tyng Cup—to the resounding chant of "J.E. Sux!"

A COLLEGIATE WAY OF LIVING

* * *

Such, my friends, is the historical answer to this query of queries. Let's turn now to the ontological issue—which will require a change of tone. To address it, I invite you to take a much longer leap back into history, to a particular moment in the life of Jonathan Edwards, the man. It is a moment to which, at this passage in my own life, I find myself irresistibly drawn. Apparently through some inescapable karma, Ginger and I are about to follow what Ross Perot has called that "giant sucking sound" coming from south of the border. We are moving to Mexico, and I shall leave this deanship that I have occupied since 1976.

On July 1, 1750, Jonathan Edwards stood before his congregation at the church in Northampton, Massachusetts, for the last time. He had served as their minister for over twenty years. Now well into midlife, he must have felt as if he were going off to a distant land to work in a foreign culture, because his next calling, though not so far away by our standards, was on the frontier, at the outpost of Stockbridge, where he was to minister to the Housatonic tribe. I am pleased to say that much of his best work was still ahead of him; but at this moment, he was looking back over his years with his congregation.

Let me simply read to you a few passages from his "Farewell Sermon," delivered on that day. Even from this distant perspective, his words are still charged with his powerful feelings of the moment. "How often," he said,

> have we met together in [this] house..., in this relation? How often have I spoken to you, instructed, counseled, warned, directed and fed you, and administered ordinances among you, as the people which were committed to my care, and whose precious souls I had the charge of? But in all probability, this will never be again...[N]othing remains, but that I bid you all farewell...I desire that I may never forget these people, who have been so long my special charge, and that I may never cease fervently to pray for your prosperity.

At this moment of departure, Edwards chose to direct himself explicitly to the young people of his congregation. "Since I have been settled in the work of the ministry, in this place," he said,

> I have ever had a peculiar concern for the souls of the young people...; and have especially exerted myself in order to it; because I knew the special opportunity they had beyond others...I have sought the good and not the hurt of our young people. I have desired their truest honor and happiness.[1]

Well, don't let me run too far with this painfully self-indulgent analogy.

There are of course many differences between the departing minister of two-and-a-half centuries ago and the departing dean of today—besides the obvious one of the immeasurably greater stature of the former. For one, Edwards puritanically warns against the "levity" and "frivolity"—I might say the "spirit"—to which youth is prone, the very spirit that surely infuses "J.E. Sux." But his "Farewell Sermon" concludes, nevertheless, with some advice that just as surely bears on my theme.

In leaving his congregation, Edwards chose to emphasize the "vast importance," the centrality, of their community life. He expressed that advice negatively, admonishing them to avoid "contention." "A contentious people," he said, "will be a miserable people." But his message, essentially, was that the welfare of the congregation depended on its internal closeness and harmony, and on its members' support of one another. That welfare, in short, depended on the congregation's value as a place of nurture.

And that, believe it or not, brings me to the ontological meaning of "J.E. Sux." It is curious that *sucking* has acquired a bad name, that it is now our preferred term of opprobrium. The images that might underlie that connotation, I ask you not even to contemplate. Search the roots of the word more deeply, I would argue, and you will find a very different meaning and a far different connotation. Despite the college's adopting the term in mock combat, that deeper meaning, in fact, is the very opposite of contention.

The psychiatrist Carl Hammerschlag points out in a recent essay that *sucking* is the ultimate image of nurture: we enter the world by sucking air, nurtured by our environment; we are sustained in it by sucking milk, nurtured by our connection with humanity. The etymology may be different, but I think of the word's homonymous relation to *succor*, to provide aid and support, to give assistance, especially in time of need.

It used to be that *to suck* was a transitive and not an intransitive verb: one sucked *something*. "The task in our lives," writes Hammerschlag, "is to find good things to suck from. Something that…fulfills us, sustains us." And those things, he suggests, are found in community, in our connections with one another—such as the connections that, year after year, are formed in this college. "This is how we thrive…," he concludes, "building community, weaving relationships—getting connected. That," he writes, is "what sucking is about. Fill your spirits with it."[2]

I hope you forgive me if, inspired by the man whose birthday we celebrate, I have turned to sermonizing—and worse, have stretched a metaphor beyond what any of us think it should be allowed to bear. But when I look back on my twenty plus years in this congregation, it is its sucking in Hammerschlag's sense—the connectedness, the relationships, the mutual support—that looms largest in my mind. Throughout that time, J.E. has had a reputation among Yale colleges for a particular intimacy, a particularly strong sense, I like to think, of community. That, I believe, has been its distinctive character. In that time, we may not always have been free of contention, but I have had many an occasion to admire the J.E. students' mutual connection and support as they have rallied around one another in crises; as the musicians among them, for example, have turned out time and again to applaud one another; or when I hear, as I did last month, of the wedding plans of two of them five years after their graduation.

Personally, I have benefited greatly from that support from other administrators, from Master Berny and Norma Lytton and their predecessors; and it has been the high privilege of my professional life to have had the opportunity, in some small way, to offer it—to "minister," if I might use that word—to the approximately 2,500 students who have been through the college in my tenure, facing crises, making discoveries, getting educated, dealing with one another, bringing "levity" and "frivolity" to this hall, and moving more deeply into their lives.

Most of those 2,500 students are gone from here now, following out their destinies in what appear to be rich and productive lives. Some have attained a measure of fame, and a few of them, alas, have died. But the college community lives on. This is "how it thrives—building community, weaving relationships— getting connected. That's what sucking is about. Fill your spirits with it." As long as the college lives on, thrives, fills its spirits in that way, then no matter what distant lands I travel to or what foreign cultures I labor in, I shall delight in my remembered associations with it. And I shall be proud to stand up and say before all the world, "J.E. Sux!"

1 Jonathan Edwards, "Farewell Sermon," in *Jonathan Edwards: Representative Selections, with Introduction, Bibliography, and Notes,* ed. Clarence H. Faust and Thomas H. Johnson, (New York: Hill and Wang, 1962), 186–202.

2 Carl A. Hammerschlag, M.D., *The Theft of the Spirit* (New York: Simon and Schuster, 1993), 119 ff.

Epilogue

Internationalizing Residential Colleges

AN EXPERIENCE IN MEXICO

In 1997, at the invitation of the rector of the Universidad de las Américas-Puebla, I came to Mexico to help establish the first residential college system in Latin America. This is an account of that project.

ONE BY ONE, to the exuberant cheers of students, the flags of the three new residential colleges at the Universidad de las Américas-Puebla were raised into the air, waving briskly under the bright Cholula sun. That gesture capped the *Ceremonia de Nombramiento* of February 27, 1998, in which the colleges, referred to only as *Colegios I, II*, and *III* during their formation, officially were bestowed with names and with all the traditional symbolism of a college — colors, coats of arms, flags and standards. Faculty selected for the newly formed college fellowships paraded in stoles, followed by students in elegant tee-shirts, all sporting the shields and warm colors of their respective colleges. Before a University-wide assembly, the rector underscored the significance of this "historic day in the life of the University," explaining his vision of the college system and alluding to its ancient roots in the medieval university. The dean of the colleges amplified eloquently on those themes, noting the system's particularly deep roots at Oxford and Cambridge universities in England. A congratulatory letter was read from the president of Yale University, which had provided a model of a residential college system and which had pledged to be a "godfather" to this project; and children of the now deceased *patrones*, the distinguished figures for whom the colleges were named, delivered moving remembrances of their newly memorialized parents. In proper ritualistic fashion, the rector formally pronounced the colleges' new names, then bestowed maces on their faculty heads and standards on their student representatives. The University chorus solemnified the occasion with a performance of Palestrina's "Gloria," and finally the newly designed flags rose to snap in the midday wind.

A special photographic exhibition had been set up for the occasion, displaying the University's history, its evolution into perhaps the premiere private institution of higher education in Mexico. After a reception and ceremonial meal, the rector and other University officials marched to each college in turn, to unveil the sign and carved stone shield that now marked its entrance. They cut ribbons to open reading rooms newly furnished with memorabilia related to the individual *patrones* and witnessed ceremonies investing the colleges' fellows and student governments with their privileges and powers. This day-long *Ceremonia de Nombramiento* was not only a kind of baptism of the colleges; it marked their emergence as full collegiate institutions and announced to the world this major new element in the education offered by UDLA, as the University is nationally known.

The inspiration for this project had come, most immediately, from the north. The lively growth of interest in establishing residential colleges at universities in the United States in recent years has begun to affect the world beyond its borders. Parallel movements have taken place in other countries influenced by British educational tradition: in Canada, Australia, and in Britain itself. The creation of residential colleges at the Universidad de las Américas represents the expansion of this recent movement into Latin America—a heritage, we might say, stretching from Oxford to Cholula.

In Mexico, this effort recalls a heritage that is Hispanic as well as Anglo-Saxon. Though the collegiate structure developed most fully and lastingly in the English-speaking world, it enjoyed an efflorescence in Spain as well. By the late fourteenth century, a "Minor College" had been built in Salamanca, the oldest university in the Hispanic world; and San Bartolomé, the first of the "Major Colleges" and a model for the rest, was erected at Salamanca in 1401. Such institutions, though they did not take root in the way of the Oxford and Cambridge colleges, were a part of Spanish university life for centuries.[1] Their founders had a broad view of education that can still speak to those working in their successor institutions today. In the antique Spanish of Alfonso el Sabio, King of Spain and founder of the University of Salamanca, the educational goal was not only *"aprender los saberes"* (to learn the fields of knowledge) but *"facer vida honesta y buena"* (to forge a good and honest life).[2] Collegiate institutions, in other words, were intended not only to train the intellect, but to form character—a traditional goal of both residential college living and of the broad liberal education that, in the Anglo-American educational heritage, has long been associated with it.

INTERNATIONALIZING RESIDENTIAL COLLEGES

At the Universidad de las Américas, the ambitious undertaking to create such units—and to introduce residential colleges to Mexico—is inspired by Rector Enrique Cárdenas Sánchez, who has sensed both their educational value and the distinct flavor that they can bring to UDLA within the context of Mexican higher education. His own graduate education was at Yale, and he was encouraged to investigate the notion by a professor with experience at Harvard. Planning for UDLA's system entailed on-site visits by a team of administrators to the campuses of Yale and of Rice University, attendance at an international congress focused on "Residential Colleges and Living-Learning Units," as well as an examination of literature on the history, purposes, and various manifestations of what we might call the collegiate ideal.

In some degree, UDLA shares in the roots of the American liberal arts college. While it is very much a modern Mexican university, with many technical fields of study, it grew out of what originally was an American-founded, English-speaking small college in Mexico City—not residential, but envisioned as a small community—known as Mexico City College. Elements of that heritage survive in the University's English language requirement, its small *tronco común*, or general studies requirement, and its accreditation in the United States. When the University moved from Mexico City to its current campus in Cholula, near the bustling city of Puebla, it was laid out by American architects along the lines of an American college, in a parklike setting outside of the city—and including dormitories, as few Mexican universities do. And UDLA remains one of the few secular, private universities in the country. In the course of its subsequent development, however, it has been fully "Mexicanized" in administration, faculty, and student body. By American standards, it is no longer fundamentally a liberal arts institution; with some 7,000 students, it is a career-oriented university, as any sizable Mexican university in our times is likely to be.

The vision of the rector, however, is that by reintroducing some of the values of a liberal arts college, not through the curriculum but rather through a system of residential colleges, UDLA can serve its students in a way that both will be important to them and will promote the health of the University. It will offer students an educational experience that maximizes the advantages of contact with other students and with faculty. With the personal attention that it gives to students and with the enhanced sense of community that it offers, it will help students integrate into the University; support the achievement of their academic goals; enhance their broad intellectual development, their social skills, and their leadership abilities; and help them develop the ethical foundations of a good life. If it can enrich their educational experience in those ways, then it will attract more students, intensify their sense of belonging to the University, improve student retention, and thus make for a more robust institution.

Integrating that vision into the existing system has been a challenge, not only in garnering the resources and establishing the physical and administrative elements, but even in convincing the faculty of its value. Like their counterparts in continental Europe, Mexican universities are generally nonresidential. And with its continental European roots, Mexico's system of higher education does not assume the broad goals of an American-style liberal education. Students choose a field of concentration upon entrance, and in the five years of study for a *Licenciatura*, or undergraduate degree, they take few courses outside of it. The specialized nature of this system means that the university is even more divided along departmental lines, and departmental perspectives, than many universities in the United States. Faculty are accustomed to thinking of their educational role as imparting training in a particular field, and not in terms of such broad purposes as "forming character" or encouraging personal development.

Just as the British college system had to be adapted for use in the United States, then, the American one must be adapted to Mexico. In tailoring the system to its Mexican setting, the team working at UDLA has been making its own original contribution toward articulating collegiate goals. In such universities as Yale and Harvard, where the functions of colleges and houses are more or less assumed, little of significance has been done to rethink and articulate their role since their founding in the early 1930s. But here at UDLA, where that role must be defined anew to the University community, the educational function of colleges is being reexamined with an awareness of both historical views and modern student development theory. Internal documents have articulated the goals of the colleges in terms of premises, vision, and objectives—expressed in terms of complementarity to the missions of academic departments. The colleges are to complement the departments' roles by attending to student development, by enhancing personal and academic growth through personal interaction in smaller communities. Those communities are to reflect the full diversity of the University's population, encouraging tolerance, ethical concerns, and democratic processes. By encouraging dialogue, they promote critical thinking as well as mutual respect. By quickly integrating students into community life and offering individual attention and various forms of support, they promote academic achievement as well as personal development—goals that in the end must be complementary, just as thought is enhanced by personal maturation.

In addition, the team has designed a quantitative system of assessment to indicate fulfillment of such collegiate goals as clarifying values, integrating new students into the community, enhancing academic performance, intensifying faculty-student contact, and cultivating leadership skills. This "performance measurement plan" also outlines more specific educational purposes of the college system within the context of the University's overall strategic plan. It involves an accounting of student participation in organizations, workshops, activities, events, and counseling sessions, and it will assess student responses with annual surveys.

The creation of UDLA's colleges has been under way since 1996. The first three colleges were formed out of the University's previously existing dormitories. Two of those had a traditional collegiate quadrangular form, built around courtyards; and additional construction has now created an enclosed court in the third. Since the *Ceremonia de Nombramiento*, a fourth quadrangle—the first college to be built from the ground up—has been opened, with three-quarters of its facility now complete. As I write, a fifth college is under way, to be created out of previously existing buildings located around the historic *zócalo*, or central square, of the nearby town of Cholula. New common spaces have been built in, or are planned for, each of these colleges: when fully furnished, they will include a study hall and classrooms; a café; lounge areas and meeting rooms; a computer room; a game room and an exercise room; music practice space; a fellows' room; offices for college administrators, counselors, and student aides; and a large, multi-use hall suitable for assemblies, lectures, concerts and other presentations, and social events. A house for the faculty head and apartments for faculty residents have been included in the newly built college, and the same is planned for the others. Common spaces for the fifth college will be located in Cholula's *Casa del Caballero Aguila*, a sixteenth-century structure, previously almost in ruins, that is being restored and rebuilt for the purpose. It is the oldest existing house in this ancient town, which was a major population center long before the Spanish conquest and which boasts one of the largest pyramids in the world. The *Casa del Caballero Aguila* will give the latest UDLA college a venerable center worthy of an Oxford or Salamanca.

Together, the colleges now house over 1,700 students, over a quarter of the full-time undergraduate population, and each has additional nonresident members. Student demand to live in the colleges has been rising steadily, and the rector's vision calls ultimately for a far more residential university, with eventually as many as ten or twelve colleges on campus and in Cholula.

The faculty heads, here called *regentes,* oversee the college, its administration, and its student life. Each is assisted by a professional *adjutor,* or administrative assistant, who typically holds or is earning a master's degree in psychology, education, or a related field. Two *consejeros académicos,* or faculty advisers, spend hours each day attending to student needs and assuring that the University's support resources, from health services to tutoring to academic advising, are made available to those who need them. The efforts of these officials are supported by a team of *asesores académicos,* faculty available for advice and tutoring in specific areas such as languages and mathematics; and by a system of student *moderadores,* or peer advisers, who live in close proximity to their advisees. In addition, each college has some twenty *socios,* or faculty fellows, who typically gather for monthly dinner meetings. They currently are establishing their rituals and their various means of supporting student educational life, largely through academic and cultural presentations as well as occasional counseling. The *socios* are not only increasing student-faculty contact outside of the classroom; they are also forging additional faculty links across departmental lines and, in the process, enriching their own social life at the University. If faculty in general initially showed some hesitancy in adopting collegiate goals, the *socios* are helping to counteract it.

The students, however, needed no convincing. Universally, in my observation, students instinctively hold collegiate values, and the tendency to bond in communities may be even stronger in this gregarious Latin culture than in the United States. In UDLA's colleges, student governments, called *gabinetes,* have taken a strong role in the development of college life. Through their efforts and those of the *regentes,* the colleges have instituted programs to integrate new students into University and college life, address academic needs, arrange cultural events and sports competitions, promote social service in the neighboring communities, organize social activities, and address concerns necessarily endemic to student life, such as alcohol, sexuality, and personal development issues. Through all of these efforts, the colleges aim to become something akin to extended families, involving a strong network of friendship and support among the students, as well as closer ties between students and faculty. UDLA, I might add, has an international flavor, drawing students in a typical semester from some fifteen countries through its exchange programs with more than ninety universities worldwide. The intensified contact between Mexicans and their international peers in these smaller, organized societies should lead to still stronger crosscultural ties and understanding.

INTERNATIONALIZING RESIDENTIAL COLLEGES

The colleges, in short, are striving to cultivate a sense of community, of home, in which students share a sense of belonging, both to their colleges and to the University. The long tradition of residential colleges has demonstrated the value of symbols and ritual in nurturing such a sense of community. Both elements are critical in forming a sense of continuity, which in turn is essential in enhancing student identification with the college. Much of the effort leading up to the *Ceremonia de Nombramiento,* then, focused on the development of appropriate symbols—colors, arms, flags and standards—created by a professor and students from the University's own department of graphic design.

But before the symbol, of course, comes the name. The University decided to name the colleges for individuals who had played a major role in UDLA's past, helping to shape it as an institution, and who also represented values that are integral to its mission. Such a policy, it was felt, would increase the students' sense of identity with the University and help "recapture" its history, promoting an awareness of the institutional past of a place that had not been very conscious of it. One of the initial three colleges was named for the two founders of Mexico City College; another for the rector who moved the campus to Puebla, changed the University's name, and expanded its vision; and the third for one of its most distinguished past professors, an eminent Mexican archaeologist. The fourth college is named for another distinguished past professor, one of Mexico's most eminent twentieth-century philosophers.

In close cooperation with a faculty-student committee, the design team created coats of arms, on which the flags, standards, and logos are based. In some institutions, such symbols are simply adaptations of the eponym's family coat of arms. None of those for whom UDLA's colleges are named, however, were armigerous in any way known to their families, so the symbols were invented. A deeply held value for each of these individuals was understanding between and among different cultures, and the committee wanted the arms to express that. By way of illustration, I shall speak only of the coat of arms for Colegio Cain-Murray, named for the founders of Mexico City College (see p. 149). It bears the figure of a double eagle: the beak of one of its heads holds a snake while the eye of the other looks toward a five-pointed star. The figure, in gold and white, is mounted on a field of dark blue, and its tail finishes in a fleur-de-lis. The field of blue surmounts a lower field of dark green, and the two are separated by a golden V-form, or single chevron. In the shield's frame, which is flat at the top and rounded at the bottom, are stylized Aztec figures of the sun (on the left) and moon (on the right).

Henry Cain and Paul Murray saw as a major part of their mission the promotion of understanding between Mexico and the United States. The motif of a double eagle is inspired by the two eagles on the shield of Mexico City College: one, with the snake, representing Mexico and the other, with the star, representing the U.S. The upper field of blue alludes to that color on the U.S. flag, the lower one of green to the green on the Mexican flag; their positions imply an implanting of an American institution on fertile Mexican ground. The overall shape of the shield is Spanish in origin, while the stylized sun and moon repeat a motif incorporated in the shield of UDLA, the institution that forms the framework, or environment, of the college. Student groups in each of the colleges created *lemas*, or mottoes, that would express their sense of community ideals, and the shields are intended to capture those values as well. In the case of Cain-Murray, the *lema* is *"corazon fuerte, mente clara, brazos abiertos"* (strong heart, clear mind, open arms). The fleur-de-lis is the traditional heraldic symbol of a strong heart, while the V-form alludes to open arms.

Along with their naturally strong affinity for communities, Mexicans, in my observation, have a highly developed sense of ritual and ceremony. Student *gabinetes,* for instance, have felt it incumbent to take solemn inauguration pledges, or *tomas de protesta,* with considerable formality and celebration, a scene quite unlikely at any university in the United States. That sensibility, that strong sense of community reinforced by a taste for symbol and ritual, should help energize and propel this educational experiment. The *Ceremonia de Nombramiento*, with all its fanfare, was only the first of numerous events to suggest that it is doing just that.

UDLA's colleges endeavor to create communities in which every student is cared for, in which every student is more likely to take full advantage of the educational opportunities offered by the University, in which every student develops his or her full potential—academic, social, and personal. They are a major element in the rector's stated goal of making students the *"eje,"* or "axis" of the University, and of assuring that UDLA is an institution *"donde cada estudiante cuenta como persona, con sus ambiciones y sus sueños"* (where each student counts as a person, with his ambitions and his dreams). The end result, we hope, will be something of notable value for our students, for the University, and ultimately for Mexico. Such were the ambitions and dreams so vividly expressed on that colorful February morning, when the new residential colleges of UDLA, to the cheers of their students, received the names and symbols that should mark their identities for generations to come.

1 Although residential colleges had almost completely disappeared from Spanish universities by sometime in the nineteenth century, they have been revived at several universities in the twentieth. See Pascual Tamburri and Daniele Bucci, "Medieval Tradition and Italian Innovations: Background of the Spanish Colleges since 1939" (paper presented at the International Congress of Historical Sciences, Oslo, Norway, August 2000).

2 Juan Alvarez Villar, *The University of Salamanca: Art and Traditions* (Salamanca: University of Salamanca Press, 1980), 89–94.

PHOTOGRAPHY CREDITS

T. Charles Erickson 76
Katherine Lantuch 128
Manuscripts and Archives, Yale University Library 21, 44, 45
Michael Marsland 15, 16, 27, 33, 41, 75, 97, 98, cover
Jaime Medina 150
William K. Sacco 141, 142
Visual Resources Collection, A&A Library 39
Yale University Art Gallery 34

www.ingramcontent.com/pod-product-compliance
Lightning Source LLC
Chambersburg PA
CBHW030443300426
44112CB00009B/1146